I have had the privilege of knowing Kathleen Nelson for quite some time. I have witnessed her life during the good times and the bad. She has been a student of God's Word her entire life. Her knowledge of the Bible and the experiences of life qualify her to write this book on spiritual warfare. Kathleen's first response to trials is to pray and seek guidance from the Holy Spirit. She and her late husband Eddy have been dear friends and great workers in the church for Christ. With great enthusiasm I recommend this book to help you through the storms and trials of life. The doctrine is pure Bible as well as Kathleen's heart. Get ready to receive help in your warfare.

—Pastor Allen Gregory
Cornerstone Assembly of God
Rowlett, Texas

Kathleen Nelson is gifted writer and well-grounded student of the Bible. Her efforts in writing *Spiritual Warfare* were gleaned over many years of being an active warrior in the kingdom of God. There is no doubt in my mind that the reader will be better educated and equipped to handle the attacks of the enemy wherever or whenever they happen. Few books today are written with such clarity for the "ordinary" Christian who is going through the various battles in their life. I sincerely believe *Spiritual Warfare* will change your life!

—Brian Hiatt
Associate Pastor
Cornerstone Assembly of God
Rowlett, Texas

Spiritual WARFARE

CREATION HOUSE

Spiritual WARFARE

KATHLEEN NELSON

Spiritual Warfare by Kathleen Nelson
Published by Creation House
A Charisma Media Company
600 Rinehart Road
Lake Mary, Florida 32746
www.charismamedia.com

Unless otherwise noted, all Scripture quotations are from the King James Version of the Bible.

Scripture quotations marked AMP are from the Amplified Bible. Old Testament copyright © 1965, 1987 by the Zondervan Corporation. The Amplified New Testament copyright © 1954, 1958, 1987 by the Lockman Foundation. Used by permission.

Scripture quotations marked NKJV are from the New King James Version of the Bible. Copyright © 1979, 1980, 1982 by Thomas Nelson, Inc., publishers. Used by permission.

All definitions are from *Webster's New World Dictionary Second College Edition.*

Design Director: Bill Johnson
Cover design by Nancy Panaccione

Visit the author's website: www.Kathleen-Nelson.com

Library of Congress Cataloging-in-Publication Data:
2012937897

International Standard Book Number: 978-1-61638-990-1
E-book International Standard Book Number:
978-1-61638-991-8

While the author has made every effort to provide accurate telephone numbers and Internet addresses at the time of publication, neither the publisher nor the author assumes any responsibility for errors or for changes that occur after publication.

First edition

12 13 14 15 16 — 987654321
Printed in the United States of America

DEDICATION

This book is dedicated in loving memory of my husband, Eddy Nelson, who encouraged me to fulfill my dream of writing, and in memory of Dena Gregory, who insisted I put my Bible studies in book form.

TABLE OF CONTENTS

Chapter One

THE ETERNAL PAST

The Eternal God

"In the beginning God..." (Gen. 1:1). God was not created; He is the Creator. Psalm 90:2 reads: "Before the mountains were brought forth, or ever thou hadst formed the earth and the world, even from everlasting to everlasting, thou art God." ("Everlasting to everlasting" could read, "From eternity past to eternity future.") God has always been and God will always be God. He has no beginning and no end. God was before time began. God started time.

Now, let us start at the beginning of Genesis 1:1 and go a little further: "In the beginning God created the heaven and the earth." Between the first and second verses of Genesis 1 there were other events that took place that are still affecting us today. Before we can understand spiritual warfare we need to go back and study something that happened so long ago that we do not even know the date of the event. It took place in the eternal past before time began.

This event is not found in one place in the Bible but is told by several writers in different books of the Bible. In order to understand what took place in the eternal past that is still affecting us today and brought on spiritual warfare, we will study the Scriptures.

God Created the Heavens and the Hosts (Angels)

The heavens were created by God:

> [God] that stretcheth out the heavens as a curtain, and spreadeth them out as a tent to dwell in.
>
> —Isaiah 40:22

> Thus said God the Lord, he that created the heavens, and stretched them out.
>
> —Isaiah 42:5

> I am the Lord that maketh all things; that stretcheth forth the heavens alone.
>
> —Isaiah 44:24

> For thus saith the Lord that created the heavens.
>
> —Isaiah 45:18

> That by the word of God the heavens were of old.
>
> —2 Peter 3:5

God created the hosts (angels and the heavenly creatures).

> I, even my hands, have stretched out the heavens, and all their host have I commanded.
>
> —Isaiah 45:12

> By the word of the Lord were the heavens made; and all the host of them by the breath of his mouth.
>
> —Psalms 33:6

> For by him were all things created, that are in heaven, and that are in earth, visible and invisible, whether they be thrones, or dominions, or principalities, or powers: all things were created by him, and for him: And he is before all things [eternal], and by him all things consist.
>
> —Colossians 1:16–17

> And sware by him that liveth for ever and ever [eternal God], who created heaven, and the things that therein are, and the earth, and the things that therein are.
>
> —Revelation 10:6

It is established that God always was and always will be (eternal); He is the Creator of all things in heaven and on the earth and without Him nothing was formed. (Create means to make something out of nothing or to bring something into existence.) God created all things including angels.

> Thus the heavens and the earth were finished, *and all the host of them* [angels].
>
> —Genesis 2:1, emphasis added

Angels, like mankind, were created eternal beings and will live or exist somewhere forever.

In the next section we will look at three of the angels mentioned by name and then we will study one of them closely, because through this angel sin entered the world and brought on spiritual warfare.

The Four Archangels

The Bible only mentions four angels by name. In this section we will take a closer look at three of the angels mentioned in order to get the big picture of angels and some of their responsibilities. The angels mentioned are called *archangels,* which means *chiefs.* They were over other angels and performed certain duties. God is also the God of order. God does everything in an orderly fashion, and as with man, He established order in the heavens.

There are many, many angels. The three we will talk about are Michael, Gabriel, and Lucifer.

1. *Michael* is known as the warring angel.

- He helped Daniel win the battle against Persia (Dan. 10:13, 21).
- He warred with Satan over the body of Moses (Jude 9).
- He will fight a future battle with Satan found in Revelation 12:7 and Daniel 12:1.

2. *Gabriel* is the announcing angel.

- He is the angel that appeared to Zacharias and announced that Elizabeth, his wife, would have a son. This son was John the Baptist (Luke 1:19).
- He also appeared to Joseph and Mary announcing the coming birth of Jesus (Matt. 1:20 and Luke 1:26).
- An archangel is mentioned as being a part of the saint's resurrection at the time of the Rapture and I really believe this archangel

is Gabriel. Gabriel has already announced the coming of Christ before His birth, and why should he not be the one to announce Christ's coming to meet the saints in the clouds (1 Thess. 4:16–17)?

3. *Lucifer* is the third angel we want to talk about. We will need to go into more detail about Lucifer in order to establish where sin came from and why there is spiritual warfare in the world. In the next section we will begin by looking at the scriptures about who he is and the event that actually changed the world.

4. *The fourth angel* mentioned in the Bible is found in Revelation 9:1, 11.

- *Abaddon* (means *the place of destruction*) is his Hebrew name.
- *Apollyon* (means *destroyer*) is his Greek name, and he is the angel of the bottomless pit.

Lucifer Created Perfect

We find in Isaiah 14:12 that Lucifer was called "*son of the morning.*" In Ezekiel 28:12–17 there is more information about Lucifer. Verse 12 says, "you seal up the sum," meaning *Lucifer was a perfect beauty and a perfectly completed pattern, a perfectly created heavenly creature.* The precious stones that covered him were: *sardius, topaz, and the diamond, the beryl, the onyx, and the jasper, the sapphire, the emerald, and the carbuncle, and gold,* listed in verse 13. No wonder he was called "son of the morning." Verse 14 says he was an *anointed cherub that covered* (*covered means to protect*), which indicates that he was in charge of someone or something. He was allowed *upon the holy mountain of God*, and also to *walk up and down in the midst of the stones of fire*. He *was perfect in his ways from the day he was created*, verse 15 says.

Yes, Lucifer was a perfect, beautiful creation of God. We will look closer at what happened. The choice he made brought spiritual warfare into the world.

Lucifer's Fall

According to what we have been told in the Bible, God's written Word, when God created the heavens and all the host of heaven everything was beautiful and perfect. But the angels and heavenly creatures like mankind were given freedom of choice. God ordained this because He wants all His creation to respect, adore, and worship Him and Him alone. From the eternal past, after He created the heavens and the host of heaven, until today, God wants all of His creation to serve Him and Him only. Remember Lucifer was an angel created perfect and beautiful. One of the questions we would ask is, What caused God to say to Lucifer, "*You have sinned*"? Another question would be, What happened to Lucifer when he sinned? How Lucifer sinned and what happened to him had a big impact not only on Lucifer's life but also on all creation in existence then and now. Lucifer's sin brought on spiritual warfare.

Ezekiel 28:12–15 says Lucifer was perfect in his ways until iniquity was found in him. *Iniquity means wickedness*. Verse 16 says, "You have sinned," so something

Lucifer thought in his heart took root and caused Lucifer to sin.

Let's look at exactly how Lucifer sinned:

> Thine heart was lifted up because of thy beauty, thou hast corrupted thy wisdom by reason of thy brightness.
>
> —Ezekiel 28:17

Notice that the sin started in Lucifer's heart, the center of all emotions of not only mankind but also in heavenly beings. Not the heart that pumps our human blood, but all creation has a heart, a spirit within that controls our emotions and helps make us who we are. We find that his heart was lifted up because of his beauty. Lucifer became conceited because of his beauty. Lucifer was called son of the morning because remember all the precious stones used in creating him. He was a beautiful created heavenly being. Because of his beauty and brightness, verse 17 says, "You have corrupted your wisdom." No longer was he making wise decisions and choices, but he lost all sense of good thinking and reasoning. He became self-centered and evil, which led to his downfall.

Ezekiel 28:16 says, "By the multitude of thy merchandise they have filled the midst of thee with violence." The Amplified Bible verse reads: "Through the abundance of your commerce you were filled with lawlessness and violence, and you sinned." The very heart of him was filled with violence and wickedness and his deeds became evil and destructive. Verse 18: "Thou hast defiled thy sanctuaries by the multitude of thine iniquities, by the iniquity of thy traffick." This word *traffick* means trade. The Amplified Bible reads: "You have profaned your sanctuaries by the multitude of your iniquities and the enormity of your guilt, by the unrighteousness of your trade." Lucifer's heavenly domain became a den of evil doings.

Now to get an even better look at Lucifer's sin and what caused his downfall, let's look at what I call "Lucifer's I Wills." There are five of them found in Isaiah 14:13–14.

For you have said in your heart:

1. I will ascend into heaven.
2. I will exalt my throne above the stars of God.
3. I will sit also upon the mount of the congregation, in the sides of the north.
4. I will ascend above the heights of the clouds.
5. I will be like the most High.

Notice Lucifer's sin started in his heart. Notice also what he said: "I will, I will, I will." This is where all sin starts; in the heart, with "I." We decide. The decisions are ours.

Now let's look at "God's I Wills."

> For man looketh on the outward appearance, but the Lord looketh on the heart.
>
> —1 Samuel 16:7

> Ye have sinned against the Lord: and be sure your sin will find you out.
>
> —Numbers 32:23

We may think we are getting by, but don't kid yourself; sin has a payday. God knew Lucifer's sin. There are five "God's I Wills" found in Ezekiel 28:16–18 concerning Lucifer:

1. I will cast you as profane out of the mountain of God. [*Profane means desecrate; defile, make common.*]
2. I will destroy you, O covering cherub, from the midst of the stones of fire.
3. I will cast you to the ground.
4. I will lay you before kings, that they may behold you.
5. I will bring you to ashes upon the earth in the sight of all them that see you.

He set himself up for the fall, and he did fall. Because of Lucifer's evil activities in his heavenly domain, God's punishment toward him was great and is still not completed. First of all God cast him out of the mountain of God, out of his heavenly sanctuary, to the ground.

> And he [Jesus] said to them, I beheld Satan as lightning fall from heaven.
>
> —Luke 10:18

We see in this verse Lucifer's name was changed to Satan. (In another section of this study we will give all of Lucifer's names used in the Bible so you can identify him easily.)

> And the great dragon was cast out, that old serpent, called the Devil, and Satan, which deceiveth the whole world: he was cast out into the earth, and his angels were cast out with him.
>
> —REVELATION 12:9

Not only was Lucifer cast out of heaven, but his angels were also. In the eternal past we see that what an angel did influenced those who were under his authority. This is evident because this passage says that his angels, the ones he was an archangel over, followed him even though his deeds were evil. When Lucifer was cast out of heaven, so were his angels. Mankind today is like some of the angels; they are easily influenced. Be careful whom you follow. God did not tolerate sin in an angel and neither does He tolerate sin in mankind. What is different for man is Jesus, who became our atonement for sin, and we can be forgiven if we repent.

Because of Lucifer's sin, darkness now covers the earth and Lucifer became *prince of the power of the air.* Genesis 1:2 says, "And the earth was without form, and void; and darkness was upon the face of the deep." What a change took place because one angel, created by God perfect, became conceited and wanted to be higher than his Creator. Sin brings corruption and it brought corruption in the heavens because about a third of the angels fell with him, and it also caused catastrophe on the earth. When Lucifer fell, sin was introduced to the heavens, and it also affects the earth today. Lucifer, or Satan as we now know him, tempted Adam and Eve in the Garden of Eden and sin entered mankind. Jesus became the atonement for the sins of man and redeemed us back to fellowship with God.

Lucifer's Names and Titles

Name	Meaning	Scripture
1. Lucifer	(son of the morning)	Isaiah 14:12
2. Satan	(adversary)	Luke 10:18; 2 Corinthians 2:11
3. Devil	(false accuser)	1 Peter 5:8; Revelation 12:9; Ephesians 6:11
4. Thief	(a stealer)	John 10:10
5. Dragon	(a fabulous kind of serpent; to fascinate)	Revelation 12:3; Revelation 13:2
6. Serpent	(sly; cunning; sharpness of vision)	2 Corinthians 11:3; Revelation 12:9
7. Beelzebub	(prince of the devils, chief of the devils)	Matthew 10:25; Matthew 12:24; Luke 11:15
8. The god of this world		2 Corinthians 4:4
9. The prince of the power of the air		Ephesians 2:2

These are the nine names or titles that refer to Lucifer, the fallen angel in the Bible. They will help you recognize him and his deeds when you read them in the Bible.

In chapter two we will study the kingdom of darkness, the enemy, and what Satan is doing now.

Chapter Two

THE KINGDOM OF DARKNESS AND THE ENEMY

The Kingdom of Darkness

When Lucifer sinned and was cast out of heaven he became *the god of this world* (2 Cor. 4:4) and *prince of the power of the air* (Eph. 2:2). Lucifer became known as Satan or the devil. Even his names make us think of evil. Now imagine with me: between heaven, where God's throne is, and the earth, where we live, is where Satan rules and reigns. His heavenly domain was taken from him and now he has set up his kingdom between heaven and earth. We will call this the kingdom of darkness. You can see why we are in spiritual warfare; you cannot see your enemies because they are evil spirits. As we continue to study our enemies we will also learn how these evil spirits affect our everyday life and the many different ways they try to hurt or bring harm to us.

This evil darkness is still out there today even though you can't see it. It is real and we can feel the effects it has upon us. In the previous paragraph I gave two scriptures in part, but I want to give you several scriptures that will help you understand more about the kingdom of darkness.

MEMBERS OF THE KINGDOM OF DARKNESS

- Lucifer: Satan, Devil
- Fallen Angels
- Principalities: Princes, Kings
- Powers: Govern like Mayors, Governors

This is a list of Satan and his followers. Trust me, they are out to harm us. All our earthly rulers, leaders, who are influenced to do evil, are being led to do so by the members of the kingdom of darkness. We see this today especially as the Rapture of the church draws closer. Wickedness in high places is seen in many of our leaders today. Satan is out to destroy God's people. We will look at this further when we study principalities and powers.

Lucifer: Satan/Devil

The god of this world (Satan)

> But if our gospel be hid, it is hid to them that are lost...*the god of this world* hath blinded the minds of them which believe not, lest the light of the glorious gospel of Christ, who is the image of God, should shine unto them.
>
> —2 CORINTHIANS 4:3–4, EMPHASIS ADDED

> And the whole world lieth in wickedness.
>
> —1 JOHN 5:19

> Who gave himself for our sins, that he might deliver us from *this present evil world,* according to the will of God and our Father.
>
> —GALATIANS 1:4, EMPHASIS ADDED

Prince of the power of the air (Satan)

> Wherein in time past ye walked according to the course of this world, according to the prince of the power of the air, the spirit that now worketh in the children of disobedience.
>
> —Ephesians 2:2, emphasis added

Power of Satan darkness

> To open their eyes, and to turn them *from darkness* to light, and *from the power of Satan* unto God.
>
> —Acts 26:18, emphasis added

> Who hath delivered us *from the power of darkness* [to light], and hath translated us into the kingdom of his dear Son.
>
> —Colossians 1:13, emphasis added

> For we wrestle not against flesh and blood, but *against principalities, against powers, against the rulers of the darkness of this world, against spiritual wickedness in high place*
>
> —Ephesians 6:12, emphasis added

We will be studying Ephesians 6:12 more closely to learn about how the kingdom of darkness is set up.

Fallen Angels

These are the angels that were under Lucifer's leadership when he was a chief archangel in the heavens with God. When Lucifer sinned and was cast out of heaven these angels were cast out too because they sinned. Lucifer is now Satan, the devil, the chief fallen angel over all the angels who were cast out with him.

> For if *God spared not the angels that sinned,* but cast them down to hell, and delivered them into chains of darkness, to be reserved unto judgment.
>
> —2 PETER 2:4, EMPHASIS ADDED

> *The angels which kept not their first estate,* but left their own habitation, he hath reserved in everlasting chains under darkness unto the judgment of the great day.
>
> —JUDE 6, EMPHASIS ADDED

> And the great dragon was cast out, that old serpent, called the Devil, and Satan, which deceiveth the whole world: he was cast out into the earth, *and his angels were cast out with him.*
>
> —REVELATION 12:9, EMPHASIS ADDED

Everything God has, Satan has tried to duplicate. The difference is, Jesus has come that we might have hope and life, and Satan gives defeat and death. Jesus is the Light and Satan gives darkness.

> For this purpose the Son of God was manifested [*manifest* means "*to make known*"], that he *might destroy the works of the devil.*
>
> —1 JOHN 3:8, EMPHASIS ADDED

> For I am persuaded that neither death, nor life, *nor angels*...shall be able to separate us from the love of God, which is in Christ Jesus our Lord.
>
> —ROMANS 8:38–39, EMPHASIS ADDED

Principalities

Principalities are those who 1) have the office of an officer or position of a prince or principal. 2) The territory or jurisdiction of a prince or the country that gives title of a prince. 3) *An angel of the third rank.*

Just like on earth, Satan has set up his kingdom of darkness with different ranks of leadership, and members of his kingdom have the office of prince or principal. Their office or rank is used to affect the leaders on earth similar to their own rank. We see this happening many times in the Bible where satanic influence has played an important role in the downfall of a whole kingdom. Even today we see and hear of kingdoms and countries whose leaders are influenced by Satan and the members of the kingdom of darkness. This interference by Satan and his followers is what causes war and troubles among the nations. That is why 1 Timothy 2:1–2 (AMP) says:

> First of all, then I admonish and urge that petitions, prayers, intercessions, and thanksgivings be offered on behalf of all men, For kings and all who are in positions of authority or high responsibility, that [outwardly] we may pass a quiet and undisturbed life [and inwardly] peaceable one in all godliness and reverence and seriousness in every way.

It is very important that we understand that Satan and the members of the kingdom of darkness are out there in the world to kill, steal, and destroy us, and their influence is real and evil. In another chapter we will study further how we can win this battle of spiritual warfare.

> For we wrestle not against flesh and blood, but *against principalities.*
>
> —EPHESIANS 6:12, EMPHASIS ADDED

> For I am persuaded that neither death, nor life, nor angels, nor *principalities*.
>
> —ROMANS 8:38, EMPHASIS ADDED

Rulers

A ruler is one who governs or rules over or controls someone. These are the rulers in the kingdom of darkness, which Satan is over, who control people who are in charge of other people. They are influenced to do evil and to destroy whomever they can. These rulers do evil things to Christians. Kings and leaders who let the devil and the members of the kingdom of darkness use them are our enemies.

> For we wrestle not against flesh and blood, *but against...the rulers of the darkness of this world.*
>
> —EPHESIANS 6:12, EMPHASIS ADDED

> Who hath delivered us from the power of darkness, and hath translated us into the kingdom of his dear Son.
>
> —COLOSSIANS 1:13

This power of darkness is from the rulers of the kingdom of darkness who do the evil works of Satan. These evil rulers influence people under their authority to do evil things to Christians, like throwing them to the lions, bringing Jesus to be crucified, and having Christians put to death for serving God; evil things that we read about in the Bible and also read about and hear on the news today; rulers Satan uses to hinder the work of righteousness.

Powers

Another word for *powers* is *stronghold. Stronghold* means 1) possession of control, authority or influence over others, 2) one having such power, 3) an angel of the fourth lowest rank. Stronghold also means a place dominated by a particular group or marked by a particular characteristic. Satan and his followers are such a group. They are in control of the space between God's throne and earth as we studied in the fall of Lucifer. Second Corinthians 10:4 says, "to the pulling down of strong holds." These are the strongholds this scripture is speaking of, the strongholds that our enemies try to control or influence us with. Satan has given power to the members of his kingdom of darkness to control or influence us to do wrong. We will discuss the deeds of these members as we dig deeper to understand who and what makes up this kingdom of darkness. With recognition and understanding we obtain knowledge to fight and win this spiritual warfare.

> For we wrestle not against flesh and blood, but *against principalities, against powers.*
>
> —EPHESIANS 6:12, EMPHASIS ADDED

> Who hath delivered us from the power of darkness.
>
> —COLOSSIANS 1:13

The power of darkness is real, but we can and do win this spiritual warfare, as you will see as you study further.

> Who hath called you *out of darkness* into his marvelous light.
>
> —1 PETER 2:9, EMPHASIS ADDED

> Who [Jesus] is gone into heaven, and is on the right hand of God [the Father]; *angels* and *authorities* and *powers being made subject unto him* [Jesus].
>
> —1 PETER 3:22, EMPHASIS ADDED

Deeds of the Members of the Kingdom of Darkness

These are found in 1 Timothy 4:1–2:

> Now the spirit speaks expressly, that in the latter times some shall depart from the faith, giving heed to [1] *seducing spirits,* and [2] *doctrines of devils;* [3] *Speaking lies in hypocrisy;* [4] *having their conscience seared with a hot iron* (emphasis added).

The Amplified Bible says it this way:

> But the [Holy] Spirit distinctly and expressly declares that in latter times some will turn away from the faith, giving attention *to deluding and seducing spirits and doctrines that demons teach, Through the hypocrisy and pretensions of liars whose consciences are seared (cauterized)* (emphasis added).

- Seducing Spirits
- Doctrines of Devils
- Speaking Lies in Hypocrisy
- Seared Conscience

Seducing Spirits

Seduce means 1) to persuade or tempt to evil or wrong; lead astray 2) to entice, 3) lure. In our world today these seducing spirits that Satan has out there are really influencing people.

> Now the spirit speaks expressly, that in the latter times some shall depart from the faith, giving heed to [1] *seducing spirits.*
>
> —1 TIMOTHY 4:1, EMPHASIS ADDED

> But evil men and seducers shall wax [grow or increase] worse and worse, deceiving, and being deceived.
>
> —2 TIMOTHY 3:13

These verses tell what happens to people who have been deceived by Satan and those of his kingdom. God will send a strong delusion to those who believe a lie (2 Thess. 2:8–12).

> *Beloved, believe not every spirit, but try the spirits whether they are of God*: because many false prophets are gone out into the world.
>
> —1 JOHN 4:1, EMPHASIS ADDED

We must be alert and careful not to be seduced by Satan or his followers.

Doctrines of Devils

The doctrines of devils are anything that is contrary to God's Word. The doctrine might sound good, but if it doesn't line up with what the Bible says, don't believe it.

> Now the spirit speaketh expressly, that in the latter times some shall depart from the faith, giving heed to [1] seducing spirits, and [2] *doctrines of devils.*
>
> —1 TIMOTHY 4:1, EMPHASIS ADDED

> Hereby know ye the Spirit of God: Every spirit that confesseth that Jesus Christ is come in the flesh is of God.
>
> —1 JOHN 4:2

> Beloved, believe not every spirit, but try the spirits whether they are of God: *because many false prophets are gone out into the world.*
>
> —1 JOHN 4:1, EMPHASIS ADDED

> Ye therefore, beloved, seeing ye know these things before, *beware lest ye also, being led away with the error of the wicked, fall from your own steadfastness.*
>
> —2 PETER 3:17, EMPHASIS ADDED

Know the Word, study it, and hide it in your heart so that you will not be deceived by anyone that preaches or teaches false doctrines. The Holy Bible is God's Word and God has preserved it from the time it was written to today, and He says His Word will never pass away.

> Heaven and earth shall pass away, but my words shall not pass away.
>
> —MATTHEW 24:35

> Study to shew thyself approved unto God, a workman that needed not to be ashamed, rightly dividing the word of truth.
>
> —2 TIMOTHY 2:15

> Whom shall he teach knowledge? and whom shall he make to understand...For precept must be upon precept, precept upon precept; line upon line, line upon line; here a little and there a little.
>
> —ISAIAH 28:9–10

I must add the next verse: "For with stammering lips and another tongue will he speak to this people" (Isa. 28:11). This verse is the key to understanding the deeper things of God. See 1 Corinthians 2:10: "God has revealed them unto us by his Spirit." Not through false teachings and false doctrines, but by the Spirit of Truth, who is the Holy Spirit.

Speaking Lies in Hypocrisy

Satan and his followers pretend to be what they are not. They are hypocrites and they are out to deceive us. *Hypocrisy means 1) play a role, 2) pretending to be what one is not or to believe what one does not, 3) false assumption of an appearance of virtue or religion.* Not only are Satan and his followers hypocrites, but also anyone who *pretends* to believe the Bible but only uses it for monetary gain or self promotion.

> Now the spirit speaketh expressly, that in the latter times some shall depart from the faith, giving heed to [1] seducing spirits, and [2] doctrines of devils; [3] *Speaking lies in hypocrisy.*
>
> —1 Timothy 4:1–2, emphasis added

> Feed the flock of God which is among you, taking the oversight thereof, not by constraint, but willingly; *not for filthy lucre* [money], *but of a ready mind.*
>
> —1 Peter 5:2, emphasis added (See also Titus 1:7; 1 Timothy 3:3, 8)

Christian leaders are worthy of their hire but should not use ungodly practices to get monetary gain. Hypocrites can be people or Satan and his followers who use ungodly ways for ungodly gain. The whole second chapter of the Book of 2 Peter talks about false teachers and doctrines. We must be careful whom we listen to and what we believe.

Satan and his followers are not only hypocrites but they are liars. In fact, Satan is the father of lies. The first lie was in the Garden of Eden when Satan, the devil, used the snake to lie to Eve in Genesis 3:1.

> Ye are of your father *the Devil....for he is a liar, and the father of it.*
>
> —JOHN 8:44, EMPHASIS ADDED

> And no marvel: for Satan himself is transformed into an angel of light.
>
> —2 CORINTHIANS 11:14, EMPHASIS ADDED

Satan is a hypocrite, which in itself is a liar. He pretends to be an angel of light, but he is a fallen archangel over the kingdom of darkness, and we must be very careful that we are not deceived by him or his followers.

Seared Conscience

> Now the spirit speaketh expressly, that in the latter times some shall depart from the faith, giving heed to [1] seducing spirits, and [2] doctrines of devils; [3] Speaking lies in hypocrisy, [4] *having their conscience seared with a hot iron.*
>
> —1 TIMOTHY 4:1–2, EMPHASIS ADDED

One of our greatest enemies can be our self. We can want something so badly that we, with Satan's help, cause our self to believe that something is right even though we know in our heart it is wrong.

This is a seared conscience: to believe something wrong is right. That is the reason we must be careful of what we try to justify even though God's Word tells us it is wrong, or we know doing certain things can lead to sin or can harm us. The meaning of *conscience* is *1) knowing or feeling, 2) able to feel or think, 3) aware and 4) knowing what one is doing and why. Seared* means *1) to make callous or unfeeling* and *2) harden*. Romans 2:15 (AMP) says, "They show that the essential requirements of the Law are written in their hearts and are operating there, with which their *consciences* (*sense of right and wrong*) also bear witness; and their [moral] decisions (their arguments of reason, their condemning or approving thoughts) will accuse or perhaps defend and excuse [them]" (emphasis added).

Our conscience cannot be our guide because our conscience is not fully reliable. A conscience can be trained in a wrong way. There is a big difference between our conscience being our guide and the Holy Spirit being our guide. *The Holy Spirit will only convict us if what we do or say is contrary to God's Word.* Our conscience can line up in agreement with the Holy Spirit; read Romans 9:1.

The Amplified Version uses the word *cauterized, and that implies that we can brand our conscience so that it no longer has any affect on us because it becomes sterilized so that our conscience does not function in a normal way.*

Listed here are some types of consciences the Bible speaks of:

- Defiled conscience (Titus 1:15)
- Evil conscience (Heb. 10:22)
- Clear conscience (Acts 24:16)
- Good conscience (Acts 23:1)
- Purged conscience (Heb. 9:14)

In order for us to stop Satan and the members of the kingdom of darkness from influencing our conscience we must do what Hebrews 13:18 says: "Pray for us: for we trust we have a good conscience, in all things willing to live honestly." We need to pray for one another that our conscience doesn't become seared. It is sad that Satan will not only use the members of the kingdom of darkness to influence us, but will use us to hurt one another.

The Enemy

Now that we have established that Lucifer's fall started spiritual warfare, we need to focus on how Lucifer's being cast out of heaven affects us. We also looked at the names in the Bible that refer to Lucifer so that we can recognize when the Word of God speaks of him. Let's turn our attention to what Satan is doing now. As he is our main enemy, we need to be aware of what he does that harms us. He deceived Adam and Eve in the Garden of Eden, but what is he doing now to hurt and destroy us today?

Satan: What He Is Doing Now?

Satan walks around on the earth seeking whom he may devour.

> And the Lord said unto Satan, whence comest thou? Then Satan answered the Lord, and said, *From going to and fro in the earth, and from walking up and down in it.*
>
> —Job 1:7, emphasis added

> Again there was a day when the sons of God came to present themselves before the Lord, and Satan

came also among them to present himself before the Lord. And the Lord said unto Satan, from whence comest thou? And Satan answered the Lord, and said, *From going to and fro in the earth, and from walking up and down it.*

—Job 2:1–2, emphasis added

Your adversary the devil, as a roaring lion, *walketh about, seeking whom he may devour.*

—1 Peter 5:8, emphasis added

Satan is like a thief; he comes to kill, steal, and destroy.

The thief comes not, but to steal, and to kill, and to destroy.

—John 10:10

Lest Satan should get an advantage of us: for we are not ignorant of his devices.

—2 Corinthians 2:11

Satan tries to deceive God's people.

And no marvel; for *Satan himself is transformed into an angel of light.*

—2 Corinthians 11:14, emphasis added

But though we, or *an angel from heaven,* preach any other *gospel* unto you than that which we have preached unto you, let him be accursed.

—Galatians 1:8, emphasis added

Stand against the *wiles of the devil.*

—Ephesians 6:11, emphasis added

> And the *great dragon* was cast out, that *old serpent*, called the *Devil,* and *Satan,* which *deceiveth the whole world.*
>
> —REVELATION 12:9, EMPHASIS ADDED

> And the devil that deceived them.
>
> —REVELATION 20:10

Satan is constantly accusing Christians before God's throne.

> For the *accuser of our brethren* is cast down, which *accused* them before our God day and night.
>
> —REVELATION 12:10, EMPHASIS ADDED

> Ye are of your father the *devil,* and the lusts of your father ye will do. He was a murderer from the beginning, and abode not in the truth, because there is *no truth in him. When he speaketh a lie, he speaketh of his own: for he is a liar, and the father of it.*
>
> —JOHN 8:44, EMPHASIS ADDED

Satan hinders Christians.

> And he shewed me Joshua the high priest standing before the angel of the Lord, and *Satan standing at his right hand to resist him.*
>
> —ZECHARIAH 3:1, EMPHASIS ADDED

> Wherefore we would have come unto you, even I Paul, once and again; *but Satan hindered us.*
>
> —1 THESSALONIANS 2:18, EMPHASIS ADDED

Satan is the tempter.

> For this cause, when I could no longer forbear, I sent to know your faith, lest by some means the

> *tempter have tempted you*, and our labor be in vain.
>
> —1 THESSALONIANS 3:5, EMPHASIS ADDED

> That Satan tempt you not for your incontinency.
>
> —1 CORINTHIANS 7:5

Satan is a distracter.

> [And *I am distracted*] *at the noise of the enemy*, because of *the oppression and threats of the wicked*; for they would cast trouble upon me, and in wrath they persecute me.
>
> —PSALM 55:3, AMP, EMPHASIS ADDED

If Satan can't stop you from doing the Lord's work, he will do everything he can to distract you.

Satan: What Is His Future?

I want to give two scriptures that tell us that Satan's future has already been determined by God:

> Then shall he say also unto them on the left hand, Depart from me, ye cursed, into *everlasting fire, prepared for the devil and his angels.*
>
> —MATTHEW 25:41, EMPHASIS ADDED

> And the *devil that deceived* them was cast *into the lake of fire and brimstone*, where the beast and the false prophet are, and *shall be tormented day and night for ever and ever.*
>
> —REVELATION 20:10, EMPHASIS ADDED

Next we will study where the battle takes place. Remember, this is a spiritual battle; so where is this battle fought?

Chapter Three

THE BATTLEFIELD

Every battle that takes place has a battlefield or a place where the battle is fought. Since we're talking about a spiritual battle, where does it take place? In this chapter we will study about where this spiritual battle is fought.

There are four main places this spiritual battle takes place. They are 1) our *minds*, 2) our *hearts*, 3) our *mouths*, and 4) *the world*. We will look at what effects our minds, hearts, mouths, and the world have on this spiritual war. According to God's Word this is where our battles take place. This is where we are temped by the devil so we will lose the battle against him and the members of the kingdom of darkness. He is our enemy and we need to know as much as possible to win this war. The Bible gives us enough information so that we can win the war against our enemies. Second Corinthians 2:11 says, "Lest Satan should get an advantage of us: for we are not ignorant of his devices." This series of lessons will help you have an advantage over Satan and his forces.

We just finished studying who our enemies are (Satan and the members of the kingdom of darkness), but how do they war against us? They, the enemies, use our *minds, hearts, mouths, and the world* as a ploy to fight against us. (*Ploy means an action or maneuver intended to outwit or disconcert another person.*) If they can maneuver us or trick us through any or all of these areas of our lives they will defeat us, but the Word says, greater is He (Jesus) that is in us than he (Satan) that is in world (1 John 4:4). We can win this spiritual war. God is on our side.

Now let us look at how Satan and his forces use our minds, hearts, mouths, and the world to cause us to feel defeated. If we understand his techniques we can be on the alert and, using what the Word of God says, win this spiritual battle.

OUR MINDS: OUR THOUGHTS

> For to be *carnally minded is death*; but to be *spiritually minded is life and peace.*
>
> —ROMANS 8:6, EMPHASIS ADDED

Our mind is where we feel, perceive, think, and where our wills and reasons come from. We cannot see our mind; it is a spirit, but it is a part of us.

Carnally Minded

Carnal means fleshly; earthy, worldly, or temporal. Romans 8:6–8 says, "*For to be carnally minded is death*; but to be spiritually minded is life and peace. *Because the carnal mind is enmity against God*" (emphasis added). *Enmity* means *enemy: deep-rooted mutual hatred.* A carnal mind is an ungodly way of thinking. *So then they that are in the flesh cannot please God.* Romans 8 is a good chapter to read to understand the difference between being carnal and spiritually minded.

> Be not conformed to this world: but be ye *transformed by the renewing of your mind*, that ye may

> prove what is that *good, and acceptable, and perfect, will of God.*
>
> —Romans 12:2, emphasis added

Our carnal minds must be transformed by God to think what is good and acceptable, and want the perfect will of God.

God Gives Us a Sound Mind

To be a *Christian means I am a Christ follower and I identify with Him.* I let Him transform me into what He wants me to be and I want to please Him, be like Him, and also think like Him. I become a new creature, from my carnal way of thinking to a spiritual way of thinking, which is Christlike. We have to want to be Christlike, to have the mind of Christ, which is pleasing to the Father.

> For God hath not given us the spirit of fear; but of power, and of love, and of a *sound mind.*
>
> —2 Timothy 1:7, emphasis added

> For who hath known the mind of the Lord, that he may instruct him? But we have the *mind of Christ.*
>
> —1 Corinthians 2:16, emphasis added

> Let nothing be done through strife or vainglory; but in *lowliness of mind* let each esteem other better than themselves. Look not every man on his own things, but every man also on the things of others. *Let this mind* be in you, which was also in Christ Jesus.
>
> —Philippians 2:3–5, emphasis added

Three Sources Thoughts Come From

Where do our thoughts come from? Our thoughts come from three sources: *1) our self, 2) the enemy,* and *3) God*. Our thoughts get their start from our hearts. We will be covering this subject closely in the next section. Let's look at what the Bible has to say about our thoughts, the enemy's input and God's.

Our Thoughts: Flesh, Human

Since we are born into the human race we think fleshly thoughts. We naturally think as humans. We are human. The fleshly thoughts we war with affect every phase of our lives. Our thoughts motivate us to do either the right things or the wrong things. Because we are in spiritual warfare we must be careful how we handle our fleshly thoughts. So do we carry through or do we disregard the thought we have? The Bible explains our different thoughts and where they come from. That is what we are talking about in this section. Our thoughts are just that, our own thoughts, and come from our own heart.

> For as he [man] thinks in his heart, so is he.
>
> —PROVERBS 23:7, NKJV

> For to be carnally minded is death.
>
> —ROMANS 8:6

Controlling Our Thoughts

What I think about is important and affects the decisions I make. What I do with my thoughts is important and affects the outcome of my thoughts. God has given to us the freedom of choice. God gives us the ability to control our thoughts but at the same time He allows us the freedom to choose and to reject the thoughts that can hurt us or others.

> *Casting down imaginations*, and every high thing that exalteth itself against the knowledge of God, and *bringing into captivity* [control] *every thought* to the obedience of Christ.
>
> —2 Corinthians 10:5, emphasis added

> And even as *they did not like to retain God in their knowledge*, God gave them over to a reprobate mind, to do those things which are not convenient [God allows people to control their own minds].
>
> —Romans 1:28, emphasis added

> *Let this mind be in you, which was also in Christ Jesus.* [This verse says we must let Christ rule our mind and thoughts.]
>
> —Philippians 2:5, emphasis added

> Thou [God] wilt *keep him [man] in perfect peace, whose mind is stayed on thee [God]*: because he [man] trusteth in thee [God]. [God is our everlasting strength.]
>
> —Isaiah 26:3–4, emphasis added

Things We Should Think On

Philippians 4:8 says *think on these things:*

Whatsoever things are:

- True
- Honest
- Just

- Pure
- Lovely
- Of Good Report
- Of Any Virtue
- Of Any Praise

What we think on is very important. Remember this verse, Proverbs 23:7—"For as he (man) thinks in his heart, so is he" (NKJV). How we handle our thoughts determines who we are and what we do.

The Enemy Thoughts: Evil

Remember our enemies are spirits. We cannot see them but we can feel their evilness. I want to give you an example of one of the ways the enemy influences us: someone says or does something that hurts you, and one of the first things you want to do is retaliate. That thought enters our mind, but where does that type of thinking come from? It could come from fleshly (carnal) thinking or it could be from a member of the kingdom of darkness. God would never tell us to retaliate. So the best way for us to handle these situations is to ask our self, Where is the thought coming from? First Corinthians 13:5 says, "think no evil." We must constantly fight these bad thoughts Satan and our other enemies would fill our minds with.

In Matthew 16:20–23 we read where Jesus was explaining to the disciples that He would be killed and then be raised from the dead on the third day. Peter began to rebuke Jesus saying, "Be it far from thee, Lord: this shall not be unto thee," but Jesus turned, and said unto Peter, "*Get thee behind me, Satan: thou art an offense unto me: for thou savourest not (savourest not* means *not mindful) the things that be of God, but those that be of men*" (emphasis added). Jesus was not calling Peter Satan but was stating a fact that Satan had deceived him from understanding the truth of what Jesus was saying. Satan can cause us to misunderstand things so that we believe lies.

Note: To refresh your memory go back and look at the section in chapter 2, "What is Satan Doing Today?" Not only is Satan doing these evil things, but so are the members of the kingdom of darkness. We need to be careful of what we think about.

> Neither give place to the devil.
>
> —EPHESIANS 4:27

> See that *none render evil for evil unto any man*; but ever follow that which is good, both among yourselves, and to all men.
>
> —1 THESSALONIANS 5:15

> Give none occasion [*chance or opportunity*] to the adversary to speak reproachfully.
>
> —1 TIMOTHY 5:14

Satan will use our thoughts and minds as an opportunity to cause us to speak and think bad things. We must not allow him to do so.

In Exodus 7:10–12 is the story of Moses and Aaron going before Pharaoh with Aaron's rod. When Aaron cast his rod down it turned into a serpent. Then Pharaoh called his wise men and his sorcerers in, and they chanted and cast their rods down. Their rods became serpents too; *but Aaron's rod swallowed up all their rods that had turned to serpents.*

Satan has power, but notice Aaron's one rod swallowed up *all* of their rods (which was a lot more than Aaron's one). Satan has power *but God is more powerful than him.* First John 4:4 says, "Greater is he that is in you, than he that is in the world." We must remember we are on the winning side. "If God be for us, who can be against us?" (Rom. 8:31).

Godly Thoughts: Godly Minded

Usually when God speaks to us or He puts thoughts in our mind or heart, it is in a still, small voice. There is a story in the Old Testament found in 1 Kings 19:11–13. God told Elijah to go stand on the mount and Elijah did so. Then *a great and strong wind* rent the mountain, *then an earthquake came, then a fire*, but the Lord was not in any of them. Then came *a still, small voice*, and the Lord spoke to Elijah.

God talked to people in the Old Testament and in the New Testament, and He talks to us today. *God never changes.*

God does speak to us but we must learn to recognize His voice. The thoughts that God puts in our mind or heart always line up with the Bible. If you have never experienced God speaking to you, you are in for a real treat, because it is so wonderful. Listen closely; God wants to talk to His people and He does.

> To be *spiritually minded is life and peace.*
>
> —Romans 8:6, emphasis added

> But he that *soweth to the spirit shall of the spirit reap life everlasting.*
>
> —Galatians 6:8, emphasis added

God's Thoughts Toward Us

> And *I will give them an heart to know me,* that I am the Lord: and they shall be my people, and I will be their God: for they shall *return unto me with their whole heart.*
>
> —Jeremiah 24:7, emphasis added

> For I know the *thoughts that I think toward you,* saith the Lord, *thoughts of peace, and not of evil,* to give you an expected end.
>
> —Jeremiah 29:11, emphasis added

> For God so loved the world, that he gave his only begotten Son, that whosoever believeth in him should not perish, but have everlasting life.
>
> —John 3:16

God's thoughts toward us can be summed up in a few words yet they are so powerful. "For God so loved the world that whosoever" that means that God loves me. Tell yourself again and again, "God loves me," because He does.

God Will Protect Our Minds

God will keep your hearts and minds through Christ Jesus (Phil. 4:7).

> Thou wilt *keep him in perfect peace,* whose *mind is stayed on thee*: because he trusteth in thee.
>
> —Isaiah 26:3, emphasis added

> *I will fear no evil: for thou art with me.* [Fear means frightening thought: an idea or thought that causes feelings of fear.]
>
> —Psalm 23:4, emphasis added

> Whosoever shall confess that *Jesus is the Son of God, God dwelleth in him, and he in God.*
>
> —1 John 4:15, emphasis added

We do not fear because God is with us and in us.

Our Hearts: Our Attitudes and Emotions

We are not talking about our physical heart, the one that pumps our blood, but our spirit heart. In the Bible this heart is called the inner man. It is the control center of all our emotions and where our thoughts, whether good or evil, take root. Notice throughout the study of our heart that most scriptures link our heart and our thoughts together. That is why we must be careful what we think about—we act on what we think.

Our Hearts: The Inner Man

> For I delight in the law of God after *the inward man.*
>
> —Romans 7:22, emphasis added

> For which cause we faint not; *but though our outward man* [flesh] *perish, yet the inward man* [inner man, spirit] *is renewed day by day.*
>
> —2 Corinthians 4:16, emphasis added

> But let it be *the hidden man of the heart, in that which is not corruptible.*
>
> —1 Peter 3:4, emphasis added

Thoughts Come from Our Hearts: Good and Bad

> *For out of the heart proceed evil thoughts,* murders, adulteries, fornications, thefts, false witness,

blasphemies: These are the things which defile a man.

—Matthew 15:19–20, emphasis added

A *good man* out of the *good treasure of his heart* bringeth forth that which is *good*; and an *evil man* out of the *evil treasure of his heart* bringeth forth that which is *evil*: for *of the abundance of the heart* his mouth speaketh.

—Luke 6:45, emphasis added

For out of the *abundance of the heart the mouth speaketh.*

—Matthew 12:34, emphasis added

God Knows Man's Heart

For man looketh on the outward appearance, *but the Lord looketh on the heart.*

—1 Samuel 16:7, emphasis added

For the word of God...is a discerner of the *thoughts and intents of the heart.*

—Hebrews 4:12, emphasis added

And *God, which knoweth the hearts...*

—Acts 15:8, emphasis added

In the day when God *shall judge the secrets of men by Jesus Christ according to my gospel.*

—Romans 2:16, emphasis added

The Amplified Version reads:

> On that day when, as my Gospel proclaims, *God by Jesus Christ will judge men in regard to the things which they conceal (their hidden thoughts).*
>
> —Romans 2:16, amp, emphasis added

> For God shall bring *every work into judgment, with every secret thing, whether it be good, or whether it be evil.*
>
> —Ecclesiastes 12:14, emphasis added

God not only knows our hearts, the very intents, but His Son, Jesus Christ, will judge us for our thoughts.

Christ in Our Hearts Makes the Difference

This spirit heart, the inner man, is where Jesus comes in and dwells and makes the difference in how our heart processes our thoughts. Christ dwelling in me also determines which side of the battle I am on. My hope is in Christ Jesus, the Captain of the winning side. In this battle there are two sides: the enemy (Satan) and God, our Father. Remember Romans 8:31, "If God be for us who can be against us?"

> That Christ may *dwell in your hearts by faith*: that ye, being rooted and grounded in love.
>
> —Ephesians 3:17, emphasis added

> Create in me a *clean heart, O God; and renew a right spirit within me.*
>
> —Psalm 51:10, emphasis added

We Must Allow God to Control Our Hearts

> And *ye shall seek me, and find me, when ye shall search for me with all your heart.*
>
> —JEREMIAH 29:13, EMPHASIS ADDED

> *Search me,* O God, and *know my heart: try me, and know my thoughts*: And see if there be any wicked way in me, and lead me in the way everlasting.
>
> —PSALM 139:23–24, EMPHASIS ADDED

> God...shall keep your hearts and minds through Christ Jesus.
>
> —PHILIPPIANS 4:7

The decision is ours. We decide who is in control of our heart. God is always ready to help us, guide us, and protect us. We need to be like Daniel and purpose in our heart that we will not defile our self, but be obedient to His will and purpose (Dan. 1:8). We can trust God with our heart. How our heart reacts in battle depends on who is in control. Our heart, as we just studied, is our control center of all thoughts and emotions, and determines what we say and what we do. We must let Jesus guard our heart.

Types of Hearts

Godly Hearts:

- Pure (Matt. 5:8)
- Clean (Ps. 51:10)
- True (Heb. 10:22)

- Humble (Isa. 57:15)

Ungodly Hearts:

- Evil/wicked (Matt. 15:19–20)
- Stony (Ezek. 11:19, 21)
- Deceitful (Jer. 17:9)
- Proud (Prov. 21:4)

Our Mouths: Our Words—What We Say

You will begin to see what is in the heart translates to our mind and comes out through our mouth. That is why we must let Jesus control our hearts.

What We Say Comes From the Heart

> But those *things which proceed out of the mouth come forth from the heart.*
>
> —Matthew 15:18, emphasis added

> For out of the *abundance of the heart the mouth speaketh.*
>
> —Matthew 12:34, emphasis added

> A *good man out of the good treasure of the heart bringeth forth good things*: and an *evil man of the evil treasure bringeth forth evil things.*
>
> —Matthew 12:35, emphasis added

We Control What Comes Out of Our Mouth

> Out of the *same mouth proceedeth blessing and cursing.* My brethren, these things *ought not so to be.*
>
> —James 3:10, emphasis added

> Let no corrupt communication proceed out of your mouth, but that which is good to the use of edifying, that it may minister grace unto the hearers. [*Edify* means to instruct or improve morally or spiritually.]
>
> —Ephesians 4:29

> But now ye also *put off all these*; anger, wrath, malice, blasphemy, *filthy communication out of your mouth.*
>
> —Colossians 3:8, emphasis added

> If any man among you seem to be religious, and *bridleth not his tongue, but deceiveth his own heart, this man's religion is vain.*
>
> —James 1:26, emphasis added

> Keep thy tongue from evil, and thy lips from speaking guile. [*Guile* means deceitful or tricky.]
>
> —Psalm 34:13

The Bible is clear according to the previous scriptures that we are to control what we say. James 3:10 says that blessings and cursing should not come out of the same mouth. Ephesians 4:29 says let no corrupt (means immoral or dishonest) communication come out of our mouth. Colossians 3:8 says we should let no filthy communication come out of our mouth. James 1:26 says we need to control our tongues. Psalm 24:13 says we must keep our tongues from evil and our lips from speaking guile (means deceitfulness). Actually, we should think before we speak and see if what we want to say will be pleasing to God.

We Are Accountable for What Comes Out of Our Mouth

We will be judged for what we say and do at the Judgment Seat of Christ. The Scriptures say we will be judged for our *words and works and rewarded accordingly.* See 1 Corinthians 3:12–15 for more information on the Judgment Seat of Christ and how we will be judged.

In Matthew 12:36–37, Jesus is speaking (emphasis added):

> But I say unto you, That *every idle word* that men shall speak, they *shall give account* thereof in the *day of judgment. For by thy words, thou shalt be justified, and by thy words thou shalt be condemned.*

> For we must *all appear before the judgment seat of Christ*; that every one may receive the things done in his body, *according to that he has done, whether it be good or bad.*
>
> —2 Corinthians 3:10, emphasis added

The Three Things James Says About the Tongue

In James 3:1–12 we find *scriptures on the tongue.* I've always found this very interesting and I want to include these scriptures in the study of our mouth and what we say. James 3:2 says, "For in many things we offend all. If any man *offend not in word, the same is a perfect man, and able also to bridle the whole body*" (emphasis added). James likens the tongue to three things. Let's look at them and learn some facts about the tongue.

Bits in a horse's mouth (v. 3)

- For obedience

- To control them
- Control of our tongues brings us into obedience to God
- If we give our reins over to the control of God, He will direct our paths

A ship's small helm (v. 4)

- Driven by fierce winds
- Guided by a small helm
- Letting God control our helm keeps us from being shipwrecked
- Letting God control us keeps us from drifting in the wrong direction

A little fire, big trouble (vv. 5–6)

- Burn a whole forest
- Cause great destruction
- Sometimes fires backtrack; be careful, you could get burned by your own careless words
- Being careful of what we say can prevent great destruction of some person's reputation

Other Facts About the Tongue From James 3

- A perfect man is one that does not offend with words (v. 2).
- The tongue is a little member (v. 5).

- It is a world of iniquity (*iniquity means great injustice or extreme immorality*) (v. 6).
- It can defile a whole church (v. 6).
- No man can tame the tongue (v. 8).
- It is an unruly evil (v. 8).
- A tongue is full of deadly poison (v. 8).

This is why we must be careful what we let into our hearts; it can go to our minds and out our mouths and do great damage. God wants to control every aspect of our lives, because He wants to guide, direct, and lead us in paths of righteousness (which means right living or living right).

> Out of the *same mouth* come *forth blessing and cursing*. These things, my brethren, *ought not to be so*.
>
> —James 3:10, AMP, emphasis added

Three thoughts from Proverbs 15:1–4:

- A soft answer turns away wrath.
- A wise tongue uses knowledge right.
- A wholesome tongue is a tree of life.

The World: Satan's Ungodly Domain

There are three (3) facts about the world that we want to study in order for us to understand other ways Satan works in our lives. One of his strategies is to tempt us to live like the world lives. It is exciting, glamorous, and fun, so it is easy to get caught up in the things of the world. Remember that *Satan is the god of this world* and that he is going *around like a roaring lion seeking whom he may devour.*

> Love not the world, neither the things that are in the world. If any man love the world, the love of the Father is not in him. For all that is in the world, *the lust of the flesh*, and *the lust of the eyes*, and *the pride of life*, is not of the Father, but is of the world.
>
> —1 JOHN 2:15–16, EMPHASIS ADDED

> Whosoever therefore will be a friend of the world is the enemy of God.
>
> —JAMES 4:4

The Lust of the Flesh

Lust is the craving for sensual gratification. It *means wanting to satisfy what our human senses crave.* Our thoughts are *centered on* the things that please *our human desires* and not on God. Human lust can cause us to sin, and sin separates us from God.

Example: Satan tempted Jesus. Matthew 4:1–11 gives the account of what we call the *temptation of Christ.* If Satan tempted Jesus, he will also tempt you and me. Hebrews 4:15 says, "For we have not an high priest which cannot be touched with the feeling of our infirmities; but was in all points tempted like as we are, yet without sin." Jesus understands temptation because Satan tempted Him, but He did not sin. Know how Jesus overcame temptation: He quoted scriptures to Satan. We need to know the Word, so we can quote scriptures when the enemy tempts us.

> But every man is tempted, when he is *drawn away of his own lust,* and *enticed.* Then when *lust hath conceived,* it bringeth forth sin: and sin, when it is finished, *bringeth forth death.*
>
> —JAMES 1:14–15, EMPHASIS ADDED

> Dearly beloved, I beseech you as strangers and pilgrims, *abstain from fleshly lusts, which war against the soul.*
>
> —1 PETER 2:11, EMPHASIS ADDED

> But put ye on the Lord Jesus Christ, and *make not provision for the flesh, to fulfill the lust thereof.*
>
> —ROMANS 13:14, EMPHASIS ADDED

> This I say then, *Walk in the Spirit, and ye shall not fulfill the lust of the flesh.*
>
> —GALATIANS 5:16, EMPHASIS ADDED

The works of the flesh are:
The works of the flesh are found in Galatians 5:16–21:

> This I say then, Walk in the Spirit, and ye shall not fulfill the lust of the flesh.
>
> —VERSE 16

> [The Spirit and the flesh war against each other] so that ye cannot do the things that ye would.
>
> —VERSE 17

> Now the works of the flesh are manifest [*manifest means to make clear or understand*].
>
> —VERSE 19

Works of the flesh:

- Adultery - immorality

- Fornication - immorality
- Uncleanness - impurity
- Lasciviousness - indecency
- Idolatry - worshiping false gods
- Witchcraft - sorcery
- Hatred - hostility
- Variance - strife
- Emulations - jealousy
- Wrath - anger
- Strife - selfishness
- Seditions - party spirit
- Heresies - peculiar opinions
- Envying - wanting what someone else has
- Murders - to kill
- Drunkenness - intoxication
- Reveling - carousing

The Lust of the Eyes

It is the greedy longings of the mind. It means ungodly longings that are sinful and destructive to man. Our eyes have been called the windows of our soul. We see and our soul or our hearts interpret what we see and how we react to what we see.

Example: Remember the story in the Bible, 2 Samuel 11–12, about David seeing Bathsheba bathing when he was walking on the roof of the king's house. She was beautiful and he wanted her, and her being married didn't stop David. He saw her, wanted her, and sent for her. In the end he had her husband sent to the front line of the battle so he would be killed, because she was with David's child and he didn't want her husband to know he was the father. Because of David lusting after another man's wife, and the fact that the child was conceived in sin, the child got sick and died. David was the king and he set a bad example; we as children of God must be careful of the example we set, as unsaved people are watching us.

> Hell and destruction are never full; so the *eyes of man are never satisfied.*
>
> —Proverbs 27:20, emphasis added

> And if *thine eye offend thee, pluck it out,* and cast it from thee: it is better for thee to enter into life with one eye, rather than having two eyes to be cast into hell fire.
>
> —Matthew 18:9, emphasis added

> The eye is the lamp of the body. So if your *eye is sound,* your entire body will be *full of light.* But if your *eye is unsound,* your whole body will be *full of darkness.* If then the very light in you [*your conscience*] is darkened, how dense is that darkness!
>
> —Matthew 6:22–23, amp, emphasis added

The Pride of Life

It is the assurance in one's resources or in the stability of earthly things. James 5:1–6 speaks of the danger of riches. We must keep our values straight. If you can remember a song I learned as a little child, it will help you to keep things in the right perspective. The song was titled "J O Y" and stood for *J*esus, *O*thers, and *Y*ou. The song says if you put *Jesus first, others second, and yourself last, you will spell JOY.*

> *Lay not up for yourselves treasures upon earth,* where moth and rust doth corrupt, and where thieves break through and steal: But *lay up for yourselves treasures in heaven,* where neither moth nor rust doth corrupt, and where thieves do not break through nor steal; *For where your treasure is, there will your heart be also.*
>
> —MATTHEW 6:19–21, EMPHASIS ADDED

> But they that will be *rich fall into temptation and a snare, and into many foolish and hurtful lusts,* which drown men in destruction and perdition. For *the love of money is the root of all evil*: which while *some coveted after, they have erred from the faith, and pierced themselves through with many sorrows.* But thou, *O man of God, flee these things: and follow after righteousness* [*right living or living right*], *godliness, faith, love, patience, meekness. Fight the good fight of faith.*
>
> —1 TIMOTHY 6:9–12, EMPHASIS ADDED

> Charge them that are *rich in this world, that they be not highminded, nor trust in uncertain riches, but in the living God,* who giveth us richly all things to enjoy.
>
> —1 TIMOTHY 6:17, EMPHASIS ADDED

> Let your conversation *be without covetousness; and be content with such things as ye have.*
>
> —HEBREWS 13:5

The last scripture I just gave is one of the key verses, because learning to be content with what we have will free us from being tempted by Satan and our other enemies to love things more than God. Here again are the scriptures I used at the beginning of this study of the world:

> Love not the world, neither the things that are in the world. If any man love the world, the love of the Father is not in him. For that is in the world, the lust of the flesh, and the lust of the eyes, and the pride of life, is not of the Father, but is of the world.
>
> —1 JOHN 2:15–16

> Whosoever therefore will be a friend of the world is the enemy of God.
>
> —JAMES 4:4

OVERCOMING THE WORLD

Paul writes to Timothy, a young man, to explain how to overcome the world and follow God (2 Tim. 2:22). Notice Paul warns Timothy about one bad thing he needs to *avoid*: "*Flee youthful lust.*"

Then Paul gives him a list of *five things* we need to *follow:*

1. Righteousness
2. Faith
3. Charity
4. Peace
5. Them that call on the Lord (fellowship with Christians) have a pure heart

In 1 Peter 2:11, Peter writes that we need to abstain from fleshly lusts (abstain means to choose not to do something). We make choices every day and we need to choose not to follow after fleshly lusts but rather to follow after the will of God. I am going to paraphrase 1 Peter 4:2:

- Live no longer for the rest of your life
- In the flesh to the lust of men
- But live to the will of God.

I also want to paraphrase Titus 2:11–12. For the grace of God that brings salvation has appeared to all men, teaching us to:

1. Deny
    - Ungodliness
    - Worldly lust,
2. We should live
    - Soberly,
    - Righteously,
    - And godly,
    - In this present world.

I want to end this part of the study of the battlefield with a list of the fruit of the Spirit. We have studied about lust, pride, and where the battle takes place (in our hearts, minds, and our mouth); but I want to end this section on a good note. Following the will of God and walking in the Spirit will lead to a victorious life and will produce the fruit of Spirit.

According to Galatians 5:22–23, the fruit of the Spirit is:

- Love
- Joy
- Peace
- Longsuffering
- Gentleness
- Goodness
- Faith
- Meekness
- Temperance

There is no law against these.

We will bear these fruits only if we follow after the things of God and if we bear these fruits we can say like Paul follow me as I follow God. First Corinthians 11:1 (AMP) says "Pattern yourselves after me (follow my example), as I imitate and follow Christ the Messiah."

Chapter 4 is a study called "Our Defense." All soldiers need to be dressed and armed ready to fight. They need to be prepared with a plan of defense.

Chapter Four

OUR DEFENSE

We have learned who our enemies are, where the kingdom of darkness is, and where the battle takes place. Now we begin a study on what is our defense. There is a lot of help we can receive if we want it. We will study how all heaven helps; God the Father, Jesus, the Holy Spirit, and angels. Remember this is spiritual warfare and cannot be fought the fleshly way. We must put on *the whole armor of God and be prepared to fight*. So what are our weapons and how do we use them? This is what this series of lessons is about.

> *For though we walk in the flesh, we do not war after the flesh*: (For the weapons of our warfare *are not carnal*, but *mighty through God* to the *pulling down of strong holds;*) Casting down imaginations, and *every high thing* that exalteth itself *against the knowledge of God*, and *bringing into captivity every thought* to the obedience of Christ.
>
> —2 Corinthians 10:3–5, emphasis added

Our Heavenly Defense

I want to explain how the Godhead, or Trinity as most Christians call the Father, the Son and the Holy Spirit, work together in perfect harmony. I call *God the Father the Master Planner* because John 3:16 says: "*For God* (the Father) *so loved the world that he* (the Father) *gave his only begotten Son* (Jesus)." Here we see that *God the Father sent His Son, who willingly came* to earth for mankind. In this spiritual battle all three are working together so that we are on the winning side.

The Father

> Thine, O Lord, is the *greatness, and the power, and the glory, and the victory,* and the majesty: for all that is in heaven and in the earth is thine; thine is the kingdom, O Lord, and *thou art exalted as head above all.* Both riches and honour come of thee, and thou reignest over all; and in thine hand is *power and might*; and in thine hand it is to *make great,* and to *give strength unto all.*
>
> —1 Chronicles 29:11–12, emphasis added

> And what is the *exceeding greatness of his power* to us-ward *who believe,* according to the *working of his mighty power,* Which he wrought in Christ, when he raised him from the dead, and set him at his own right hand in the heavenly places, Far above all principality, and power, and might, and dominion, and every name that is named, not only in this world, but also in that which is to come: And hath put *all things under his feet,* and gave him to be head over all things to the church, Which is his body, the fullness of him that filleth all in all.
>
> —Ephesians 1:19–23, emphasis added

I believe these two scriptures are talking about God the Father. All three in the Godhead have greatness, power, glory and victory but notice the passage in Ephesians says set him (Christ) at his (the Father's) right hand and put all things under his (Jesus) feet and gave to him (Jesus) to be head over all things to the church, which is his body. God the Father put all things under Christ's feet and gave to Christ to be head over the church that is the believers, the Christians. Also read the seventeenth chapter of John. This chapter contains Christ's prayer before He was crucified. Verses 4 and 5 are Jesus's prayer to His Father. Jesus says: "I have glorified thee on the earth: I have finished the work which thou gavest me to do. And now, O Father, glorify thou me with thine own self with the glory which I had with thee before the world was" (emphasis added).

The Master Planner, God the Father does not want any to perish from sin or to perish in the battle of spiritual warfare. We are winners. Jesus did complete the plan of the Father and now we have access to the throne of God the Father.

The Son

Hope has two meanings: 1) to desire or expect and 2) *confident expectation*. The second hope is the one we have in Christ. Christ is the hope of our salvation, of our future resurrection, and of us winning the spiritual warfare. We will go in more detail of Jesus's help in battle when we study the armor of God. Jesus is strong and mighty in battle and He gives us power to overcome and win the spiritual battle we are fighting now, *because greater is He that is in you, than He that is in the world.*

> Who is this King of glory? *The Lord strong and mighty, the Lord mighty in battle.*
>
> —Psalm 24:8, emphasis added

> Finally, my brethren, *be strong in the Lord, and in the power of his might.*
>
> —Ephesians 6:10, emphasis added

> Ye are of God, little children, and have *overcome them: because greater is he that is in you, than he that is in the world.*
>
> —1 John 4:4, emphasis added

The Holy Spirit

Since this a spiritual battle, what better defense can we have than the Spirit of God, the Holy Spirit? John 14:17 says in part that the Spirit of truth dwells *with* you and shall be *in* you. If we have Christ in us and the Holy Spirit *dwells* (*which means makes His home*) in us, what more do we need to help fight our spiritual battle. The Holy Spirit gives us power; power to overcome anything our enemy sends our way to tempt us or hinder us. The Holy Spirit is also our defender and will fight for us.

> When the enemy shall come in like a flood, the *Spirit of the Lord shall lift up a standard against him.*
>
> —Isaiah 59:19, emphasis added

Standard means a distinctive flag, as a military group would have. Using this meaning of standard in the context of this verse, it is saying when the enemy comes bearing down on you, the Holy Spirit will come charging at the enemy with His banner lifted high and stop him in his tracks.

> And, behold, I send the promise of my Father upon you: but tarry ye in the city of Jerusalem, until ye

> be *endued* [*endued* means *to provide with something*] *with power from on high.*
>
> —LUKE 24:49, EMPHASIS ADDED

This is Jesus speaking before He ascended into heaven. The Holy Spirit has provided the power we need for anything we need, power to overcome the impact of our enemy and to win the battle.

> But ye shall receive power, after that the Holy Ghost is come upon you.
>
> —ACTS 1:8

> May He grant you out of the rich treasury of His glory to be strengthened and *reinforced with mighty power in the inner man by the* [*Holy*] *Spirit* [*Himself indwelling your innermost being and personality*].
>
> —EPHESIANS 3:16, AMP, EMPHASIS ADDED

We will study more about how the Holy Spirit as a part of our heavenly defense when we study the armor of God.

Heavenly Angels

We already did a study on the fallen angels, now we will study about all the angels that are still a big part of God's heavenly kingdom. There are many, many angels that no man can number. We know there are herald angels, who announce important events; there are warring angels who help fight battles; and there are guardian angels assigned to watch over people. There are also ministering angels who minister to the Christians. We read in the Book of Revelation that during the tribulation a lot of angels will announce and precipitate in the judgments that will come upon the earth. The angels we will discuss in this study are the ones who minister to and deliver Christians from the evil forces of the enemies from the kingdom of darkness.

There are many stories in the Bible where angels ministered to and delivered people. When Daniel was in the lion's den an angel shut the mouths of the lions (Dan. 6:22). After Jesus was tempted by Satan angels came and ministered to him (Matt. 4:11). Acts 12:1–16 tells the story of an angel delivering Peter out of prison. These angels are still delivering, ministering, and helping people today.

> For he shall give his *angels charge over thee*, to keep thee in all thy ways. They shall *bear thee up in their hands*, lest thou dash thy foot against a stone.
>
> —Psalm 91:11–12, emphasis added

> Are they not all *ministering spirits*, sent forth to *minister for them who shall be heirs of salvation*? [These are ministering angels.]
>
> —Hebrews 1:14, emphasis added

> The angel of the Lord *encampeth round about them that fear him*, and *delivereth them.*
>
> —Psalm 34:7, emphasis added

We have a guardian angel who watches over us. God has charged His angels to camp around about us and to keep us. Do you believe that God has given angels to keep us? He has. I believe if our spiritual eyes were opened we would be so surprised to see all the activity that goes on in heaven and between heaven and earth. Nothing can compare to the heavenly force that God the Father has given to us to help fight this spiritual battle.

Armed by God

Not only do we have the heavenly Trinity; Father, Son, and Holy Spirit fighting for us, and the heavenly angels around us; God has given us spiritual weapons to use in this spiritual warfare. Remember our *weapons are not carnal* (earthly) but *mighty through God* (spiritual) to pull down the strongholds. Ephesians 6:10–18 lists the armor of God that we must put on if we are to win this spiritual warfare. We will study each of the six pieces of armor that we are to put on and use as our defense.

In order to get a better picture of the *difference between carnal and spiritual armor, let's look at the story of David trying to wear Saul's armor to fight the giant.* First Samuel 17:37–39, 43–47 relates the story. I will list the facts so you can compare:

Facts About Saul's Armor

- Saul had a helmet
- Saul had a coat of mail armor
- Breastplate
- Shield
- Belt
- Saul had a sword
- Saul's armor did not fit David

Facts About the Giant

- The giant had a sword
- The giant had a spear

- The giant had a shield
- The giant was bigger than David

Facts About David

- David had a sling
- David had five smooth stones
- David had the God of the armies of Israel
- David had the key words: "*The battle is the Lord's, and he will give you into our hands.*"

We can say, like David, the battle is the Lord's, and He will give the enemy into our hands. We will not be defeated. David knew he could not defeat the giant alone. We cannot defeat our enemy alone either, so God has given us spiritual armor to use in this spiritual battle. Remember, the weapons of our warfare are not carnal, but mighty through God. Saul's armor was carnal but our armor is spiritual, mighty, and powerful, and can pull down every stronghold (1) a fortified place: Fortress 2) A place dominated by a particular group). Satan is the god of this world and the prince of the power of the air, and his kingdom is between heaven and the earth, but we have a mighty spirit army to help fight our battle. We are dressed for battle because we have spiritual armor for spiritual warfare. We are more than conquerors (Rom. 8:37). If God be for us, who can be against us (Rom. 8:31)? We, like David, can say the battle is the Lord's.

Dressed for Battle/Armor of God

Ephesians 6:10–18 not only lists the armor of God, but this passage gives us some key words that also equip us for battle. Verses 11 and 13 list five important facts:

From the King James Bible (emphasis added):

> Put on the *whole armor of God,*
>
> That you may be able to *stand against the wiles of the devil.*
>
> Wherefore take unto you the *whole armor of God,_*
>
> That you may be able to *withstand* in the evil day,
>
> And having done all, *to stand.*

From the Amplified Bible (emphasis added):

> Put on *God's whole armor—the armor of a heavy-armed soldier, which God supplies*
>
> That you may be able *successfully to stand up against (all) the strategies and the deceits of the devil.*
>
> Therefore put on *God's complete armor,*
>
> That you may be able to *resist and stand your ground* on the evil day (*of danger*),
>
> And having done all (the crisis demands), *to stand* (firmly in your place).

In this passage of Scripture there are three key thoughts I want to cover. The word stand is used three times in verses 11, 13, and 14, and withstand is used once in verse 13.

Stand/Withstand

Stand means *1) to remain firm in the face of, 2) to participate in (a military formation). Stand* also means *1) to take up or maintain a specified position, 2) to maintain one's position, 3) to be firm and steadfast in support or opposition.*

Withstand means 1) *stand up against. 2) to resist successfully, 3) to resist the attraction or influence of 4) to stop or obstruct the course of.*

God wants us to know our position and stand firm and not be moved. We can resist successfully the devil and the entire kingdom of darkness's deceit and temptations. We cannot run. We must stand firm.

> Resist the devil, and he will flee from you.
>
> —James 4:7

> Neither give place to the devil.
>
> —Ephesians 4:27

> Watch ye, *stand fast* in the faith.
>
> —1 Corinthians 16:13, emphasis added

Be strong in the Lord

Ephesians 6:10 says, "Finally, my brethren, *be strong in the Lord*" (emphasis added). Notice here it says *be strong in the Lord*. David said in Psalm 121:2, "My *help comes from the Lord*, which made heaven and earth" (emphasis added). *Our help* is in the *name of the Lord* (Ps. 124:8). We have a powerful effect because we are *strong in the Lord*. Strong in the military sense means: 1) *well defended and difficult to capture,* 2) *a strong fortress*. This is the *strong* the Bible talks about when it says, "strong in the Lord." In Psalm 91:2, David says: "I will say of the Lord, He is my *refuge* and my *fortress*: my God; in him will *I trust*" (emphasis added). Jeremiah says it well in Jeremiah 16:19: "O Lord, my *strength*, and my *fortress*, and my *refuge* in the day of affliction."

> And he said unto me, My grace is sufficient for thee: for *my strength is made perfect in weakness*...for when I am weak, then am I strong.
>
> —2 Corinthians 12:9–10, emphasis added

> I can do *all things through Christ* which strengtheneth me.
>
> —Philippians 4:13, emphasis added

> Quit you like men, be strong. [Quit means: conduct (act manly).]
>
> —1 Corinthians 16:13

We go into this battle equipped because we go in the strength of the Lord.

Power of His might

We are made strong when we go into battle with *the power of His might* (Eph. 6:10). The power of His might is our reinforcement, our strength. This power comes from within; through Jesus Christ our Savior and the Holy Spirit dwelling in the inner man, our spiritual heart.

> May He grant you out of the rich treasury of His glory to *be strengthened* and *reinforced with mighty power* in the inner man by the [Holy] Spirit [Himself indwelling your innermost being and personality].
>
> —Ephesians 3:16, amp, emphasis added

> Now unto him [Christ] that is able to do *exceeding abundantly* above all that we ask or think, according to *the power that worketh in us.*
>
> —Ephesians 3:20, emphasis added

> Who is this King of glory? *The Lord strong and mighty, the Lord mighty in battle.*
>
> —Psalm 24:8, emphasis added

> Thine, O Lord, is the greatness, and *the power*, and the glory, and *the victory*, and the majesty: for all that is in the heaven and in the earth is thine; thine is the kingdom, O Lord, and thou art exalted as head above all. Both riches and honor come of thee, and thou reignest over all; and *in your hand is power and might*; and in your hand it is to make great, and *to give strength* unto all.
>
> —1 Chronicles 29:11–12, emphasis added

> O God, thou art terrible out of thy holy places: the God of Israel is he that *giveth strength and power unto his people.*
>
> —Psalm 68:35, emphasis added

> For God hath not given us the spirit of fear; but of *power*, and of love, and of a sound mind.
>
> —2 Timothy 1:7, emphasis added

> Ye are of God, little children, and have *overcome them: because greater is he that is in you, than he that is in the world.*
>
> —1 John 4:4, emphasis added

God's Word will not fail; He will do what He has promised us, and one of His promises is to give us His power to overcome all the enemy's tricks, temptations, and lies. We have the power in us.

The Armor of God: Dressed for Battle

There are six pieces to the armor of God found in Ephesians 6:14–17. We will study each piece separately in order to learn the purpose of each piece. Every piece is necessary, and to be fully equipped to *fight the good fight of faith* (1 Tim. 6:12) we *must put on the whole armor of God* (Eph. 6:13). We must *remember* this is a spiritual battle and our armor must be spiritual in order for us to successfully win this war. This battle is a daily warfare, so we must wear our armor at all times and be prepared to use it at any given moment. Now, get ready to dress for battle.

The Belt of Truth

First we must put on the belt of truth. Ephesians 6:14 says, "Having your *loins girt about with the truth* (the belt)" (emphasis added). *Girt means make fast, surround, to prepare oneself for action. Equip.* We must first surround our self with the truth, because knowing the truth helps us be prepared and ready for action. We must take on the character of Christ. Numbers 23:19 says, "God is not a man, that He should lie." Neither the Father, nor Son, nor the Holy Spirit can lie. Jesus cannot lie so Jesus cannot fail. We can depend on Him. Put on the belt of truth and you will be surrounded by Christ.

Jesus is the truth

> Jesus saith unto him, I am the way, *the truth*, and the life: no man cometh unto the Father, but by me.
>
> —John 14:6, emphasis added

> And *the Word* was made flesh, and dwelt among us...full of grace and *truth*.
>
> —John 1:14, emphasis added

> Grace and *truth came by Jesus Christ.*
>
> —JOHN 1:17, EMPHASIS ADDED

Jesus truth is everlasting

> For his merciful kindness is great toward us: and the *truth of the Lord endureth for ever.* Praise ye the Lord.
>
> —PSALM 117:2, EMPHASIS ADDED

> For the Lord is good: his mercy is everlasting; and *his truth endureth to all generations.*
>
> —PSALM 100:5, EMPHASIS ADDED

Jesus truth sets us free from sin's bondage

> And ye shall *know the truth,* and the *truth shall make you free.*
>
> —JOHN 8:32, EMPHASIS ADDED

> Sanctify them through *thy truth: thy word is truth.*
>
> —JOHN 17:17, EMPHASIS ADDED

The devil is the opposite; he is the father of lies.

> Ye are of *your father the devil*...and abode not in the truth, *because...when he speaketh a lie, he speaketh of his own: for he is a liar, and the father of it.*
>
> —JOHN 8:44, EMPHASIS ADDED

The devil cannot speak the truth because there is no truth in him. We cannot trust the devil—he is a liar—so wearing the belt of truth will make us aware of Satan and his lies.

The Breastplate of Righteousness

The breastplate covers the chest where the heart is located. In this spiritual battle, how does a spiritual breastplate help us? Righteousness means *1) acting rightly, 2) according to what is right; doing what is right.* Isaiah 64:6 says, "Our righteousness is as filthy rags." If our righteousness is as *filthy rags* and we need the breastplate of righteousness to protect us from the enemy, where do we get one? Romans 10:1–13 has the information we need. I suggest you read these verses but I want to sum them up for you.

- Paul's prayer: that they might be *saved* (v. 1).
- The Israelites were trying to establish their *own righteousness* (v. 2).
- They were *ignorant of God's righteousness* (v. 3).
- Paul explains *righteousness through faith*; not the law, but faith in Christ (vv. 4–9).
- Paul says it is for *whosoever*: this *righteousness* and salvation (vv. 11–13).

The key verse here I want us to look at is verse 10: "For with the heart man believes unto righteousness; and with the mouth confession is made unto salvation" (emphasis added). We need the breastplate of righteousness, and that is Christ living in our spiritual heart filling us with His righteousness. Therefore we have on the breastplate of righteousness (Eph. 6:14).

Our righteousness

> But we are *all* as an *unclean* thing, and all our righteousnesses are as fifty rags.
>
> —Isaiah 64:6, emphasis added

> And be found in him, not having mine own righteousness, which is of the law, but that which is through the faith in Christ, the *righteousness which is of God by faith.*
>
> —Philippians 3:9, emphasis added

Jesus's righteousness

> And the heavens shall declare *his righteousness*: for God is judge himself.
>
> —Psalm 50:6, emphasis added

> The heavens declare *his righteousness*, and all the people see his glory.
>
> —Psalm 97:6, emphasis added

> This is the heritage of the servants of the Lord, and *their righteousness is of me*, saith the Lord.
>
> —Isaiah 54:17, emphasis added

> His work is honorable and glorious: and *his righteousness endureth for ever.*
>
> —Psalm 111:3, emphasis added

Christ's righteousness endures forever.

First John 1:7 says, "But if we walk in the light, as he is in the light, we have fellowship one with another, and the *blood of Jesus Christ his Son cleanses* us *from all sin*" (emphasis added). (Sin is unrighteousness, which means wicked, *sinful* or evil.) We are cleansed, covered and protected by Christ's righteousness.

Feet Shod With the Gospel of Peace

> And your *feet shod with the preparation of the gospel of peace.*
>
> —Ephesians 6:15, emphasis added

The word *preparation* means 1) to make ready in advance; 2) readiness. No soldier would willingly go barefooted into a battle. They would want the most comfortable and sturdiest shoe that could be bought. God has given to us in preparation for this spiritual battle the best: His Son's blood.

> For ye are bought with a price.
>
> —1 Corinthians 6:20

The human race was separated from God because of Adam's sin. Jesus has become our sacrificial Lamb, which took down the wall (the division) between God and man; therefore Jesus has become our peace. Gospel (means good news) and the good news here is that Christ has made it possible for man to have fellowship once again with God the Father.

Jesus is our peace

> But now in Christ Jesus ye who sometimes were far off are made nigh [near] by the blood of Christ. For *he is our peace*, who hath made both one, and hath broken down the middle wall of partition between us.
>
> —Ephesians 2:13–14, emphasis added

> And, having *made peace through the blood of his cross*...
>
> —Colossians 1:20, emphasis added

Jesus gives us peace

> Peace I leave with you, *my peace I give* unto you: not as the world giveth, give I unto you. Let not your heart be troubled, neither let it be afraid.
>
> —John 14:27, emphasis added

> And let the *peace of God rule in your hearts.*
>
> —Colossians 3:15, emphasis added

Jesus keeps the saint's feet

> He will keep the *feet of his saints*, the wicked shall be silent in darkness; for by strength shall no man prevail [win].
>
> —1 Samuel 4:9, emphasis added

> [Jesus has] put *all enemies under his feet.*
>
> —1 Corinthians 15:25–27, emphasis added

Jesus blesses those who spread the gospel (good news)

In 2 Corinthians 4:3–7 we find a passage of Scriptures saying that *the god of this world* (Satan) has blinded the minds of those who believe not. If we don't tell the "good news," how will the unsaved know about the Redeemer and His work on the cross? We must spread the "good news," *the gospel of peace.* Our *feet must be shod with the gospel of peace* and we must go tell. Two scriptures follow that tell how God feels about people who tell the "good news."

> How *beautiful* upon the mountains are the *feet of him that bringeth good tidings*, that *publisheth*

> *peace*; that bringeth good tidings of good, that publisheth salvation; that saith unto Zion, Thy God reigneth!
>
> —Isaiah 52:7, emphasis added

> How *beautiful are the feet of them that preach the gospel of peace,* and bring glad tidings of good things!
>
> —Romans 10:15, emphasis added

I want to give you a scripture that has meant a lot to me down through the years: Romans 1:16, "For I am not ashamed of the gospel of Christ: for it is the power of God unto salvation to every one that believeth; to the Jew first, and also to the Greek" (emphasis added). We are privileged to have our feet shod with the preparation of the gospel of peace. Colossians 2:6 says, "As ye have therefore received Christ Jesus the Lord, so walk ye in him" (emphasis added). He is our example. Follow in His footsteps (see 1 Peter 2:21).

The Shield of Faith

> *Above all, taking the shield of faith,* wherewith ye shall be able to quench all the fiery darts of the wicked.
>
> —Ephesians 6:16, emphasis added

Above all is used to indicate the most important thing or the main point of a statement. So, above all used here indicates that the most important piece of the armor of God is the shield of faith.

Faith facts

The biblical meaning of *faith* is found in Hebrews 11:1—"Now faith is the substance of things hoped for, the evidence of things not seen." The dictionary meaning of *faith* is, 1*) trust in God, 2) belief in or trust in somebody without logical proof.* Hebrews 11 gives examples of Old Testament faith.

In Matthew 17:20, Jesus said, "If ye have faith as a grain of mustard seed, ye shall say unto this mountain, Remove hence to yonder place; and it shall remove; and nothing shall be impossible unto you" *(hence means 1) because of this or from this cause or reason, 2) away from here or away from this place).*

In this spiritual warfare *faith* is *absolutely necessary*; that is why the Bible says "*taking the shield of faith.*" We cannot go into this battle without *taking the shield of faith. Shield* means *1) a piece of armor carried on the arm and used as a protection against weapon blows 2) is a safeguard used as a safety measure. Faith* acts as a *spiritual shield* that *protects us or defends us.*

With *the shield of faith* on your arm, *you shall be able to quench all the fiery darts of the wicked.* What a powerful weapon we have been given. Notice, this scripture does not say we should be able, but it says, "you shall be able to quench *all* the fiery darts of the wicked." (*Quench means extinguish fire: to put out a fire).* In part five of this study we will look at some of *the fiery darts of the wicked* and how we can quench them. The members of the kingdom of darkness are always sending fiery darts our way, but remember we have *the Father, the Son, and the Holy Spirit, plus all the heavenly angels as our defenders; and we also have on the whole armor of God!* What a powerful defense God has given us! In this spiritual battle *we cannot see our defenders or our enemies*, but we can trust God's Word; *by faith* we know they are there to help fight our battles.

> For we walk by faith, not by sight.
>
> —2 Corinthians 5:7

> But *without faith it is impossible to please him* [God].
>
> —Hebrews 11:6, emphasis added

> God hath *dealt to every man the measure of faith.*
>
> —Romans 12:3, emphasis added

Dealt means 1) to give out; reward, 2) distribute something, to give a share of something). Measure means 1) a standard amount of something, 2) amount that is limited, suitable or reasonable. Notice the word the used before measure; it indicates that a specific amount of faith has been given to every man. Whatever the amount of faith that has been given to us, we can increase our faith.

Paul writes in 2 Thessalonians 1:3, "We are bound to thank God always for you, brethren, because that *your faith grows exceedingly*" (emphasis added). We all are given faith; we must increase our faith. First Peter 5:9 says, "Whom (the devil) *resist steadfast in the faith*" (emphasis added). God has given each of us the measure of faith so that we can stand firm, fixed in the faith, ready for battle.

Measures of faith

- *Little Faith*—Jesus to disciples—supplying needs (Matt. 6:30)

- *Great Faith*—Jesus to centurion—sending His word (Matt. 8:10)
- *No Faith*—Jesus to disciples—calming storm (Mark 4:40)
- *Weak Faith*—Paul to Christians—how to help others (Rom. 14:1)

Paul writes to Timothy in 2 Timothy 4:7, "I have fought a good fight, I have finished my course, I have kept the faith" (emphasis added). Paul fought, finished, and kept the faith. Keep the faith means do not despair regardless of what may happen. We must keep the faith. If we keep the faith we will win the battle.

Helmet of Salvation

> And *take the helmet of salvation.*
>
> —Ephesians 6:17, emphasis added

Helmet means armor for the head, a hard protected head covering. A helmet covers the head and that is where our brain is located. The brain is where our thoughts are formed and where most of the spiritual warfare takes place. Remember in Part 3 we studied that there are three sources our thoughts come from: ourselves, the enemy, and God. Our heads need a protective covering because our thoughts need protection and guidance. God has made provision for a covering for us to protect us during this spiritual warfare.

Salvation means 1) redemption, 2) the saving of the soul from sin and its consequences.

> Who [God the Father] hath *delivered us from the power of darkness*, and hath *translated us into the kingdom of his dear Son*: In whom we have *redemption* through his blood, even the *forgiveness of sins*.
>
> —COLOSSIANS 1:13–14, EMPHASIS ADDED

God the Father made provision for our salvation (redemption) through His Son. This is the salvation that is part of the armor of God; this helmet not only protects our minds and thoughts, but covers us and set us apart as members of the kingdom of God and His army.

> Let us therefore *cast off the works of darkness*, and *let us put on the armor of light* [Jesus is this light].
>
> —ROMANS 13:12, EMPHASIS ADDED

> For he put on righteousness as a breastplate, and an *helmet of salvation* upon his head; and he put on the garments of vengeance for clothing, and was clad with zeal as a cloak.
>
> —ISAIAH 59:17, EMPHASIS ADDED

When a soldier puts on his helmet, he is saying, "I am ready to fight." That says he is in earnest about fighting; that he is a part of the army of God. Until we put on this piece of armor we aren't soldiers of the Cross and we are not ready for battle. The helmet we wear identifies which side we are on.

The Sword of the Spirit

> And *the sword of the Spirit*, which *is the word of God.*
>
> —EPHESIANS 6:17, EMPHASIS ADDED

One of the meanings I found for sword surprised me. Sword means 1) a long bladed weapon, 2) use of force: the use of force, violence or military power. God has given to us a spiritual weapon that has the force and power of a military weapon so that we can defeat any foe. In fact it is more powerful than any sword ever made by man, or that could ever be made by man. Let's look closely at the sword of the Spirit, which is the Word of God.

The Word of God is:

> In the beginning was *the Word*, and *the Word* was with God, and *the Word* was God. The same was in the beginning with God....And *the Word was made flesh*, and dwelt among us, (and we beheld his glory, the glory as of the only begotten of the Father,) full of grace and truth.
>
> —John 1:1–2, 14, emphasis added

Jesus was the Word of God in flesh, and the Bible is His written word.

> And he was clothed with a vesture dipped in blood: and *his name is called The Word of God.*
>
> —Revelation 19:13, emphasis added

Genesis 1:1 says, "In the beginning God created the heaven and the earth." Verses 3, 4, 6, 9, 11, 20, 24, 26, and 29 say, "and God said."

Jesus is also *the spoken Word.*

> For by him [God's Son] were *all things created*, that are in heaven, and that are in earth.
>
> —Colossians 1:16, emphasis added

Created means to bring something into existence. The Word speaks and the wind obeys, the sick are made whole, the lame walk, and battles are won. The Word of God spoke and the world was formed.

There are *five facts* about the *Word of God* found in the following scripture:

> For the *word of God* is *quick*, and *powerful*, and *sharper* than any two edged sword, *piercing* even to the dividing asunder of soul and spirit, and of the joints and marrow, and is a *discerner* of the thoughts and intents of the heart.
>
> —Hebrews 4:12, emphasis added

1. *Quick*: 1) not dead, living, alive, 2) rapid, speedy—fast in understanding, thinking, or learning.

The Word of God is quick. What better weapon could God give us than a spiritual weapon that is fast acting, prepared, and ready, and even knows exactly what will happen before it does. What makes this weapon quick is the same Spirit that will quicken our mortal bodies at the time of resurrection. Quicken means to come alive. This weapon can take action faster than a speeding bullet.

2. *Powerful*: 1) possession of control, authority or influence over others, 2) having great power.

> For the *weapons of our warfare* are not carnal, but *mighty through God* to the pulling down of strong holds.
>
> —2 Corinthians 10:4, emphasis added

The Word of God is powerful. Our weapons are not carnal; they are not man-made; they are spiritual, fast, accurate, and powerful. Not only has God given us the power to overcome the enemy, but a powerful weapon to use to fight the enemy. We will not be defeated.

3. *Sharper*: 1) adapted to cutting or *piercing*, 2) keen in *intellect*, keen in *perception*, 3) keen to one's own interest 4) keen in *spirit*, 5) set forth with *clarity and distinctness.*

> And *out of his* [Jesus's] *mouth* goes a *sharp sword*, that with it he should smite the nations: and he shall rule them with a rod of iron.
>
> —Revelation 19:15, emphasis added

The Word of God is sharper than any two edged sword. Jesus's spoken Word will defeat the enemy. Let's look at just how sharp the Word of God is: sharper than any two edged sword. A two edged sword can cut two ways: coming and going. A person using this type of weapon can cut and draw it back and cut again. Because it is also quick, this weapon can cut so fast it can accomplish what it set out to do before the enemy is aware of it.

4. *Piercing*: 1) *Penetrating*: having an unpleasantly intense quality, 2) *Perceptive*: capable of acute perception.

The Word of God is piercing even to the dividing asunder of soul and spirit, and of the joints and marrow. It penetrates and can even divide the soul from the spirit and can separate the joints and the marrow. In other words, the Word of God not only penetrates the soul, but it is perceptive so it knows where and what to target every time. We can depend on the Word of God to zero in on the problem and also have the solution.

5. *Discerner*: One that can accurately read character or motives.

The Word of God is a discerner of the thoughts and intents of the heart. The Word of God knows us, knows the enemy, and accurately knows the motives of all people and all the enemies in the kingdom of darkness. There is nothing hidden from the Word.

> A *good man* out of the *good treasure of his heart* brings forth that which is *good*; and an *evil man* out of the *evil treasure of his heart* bringeth forth that which is *evil*: for *of the abundance of the heart* his mouth speaketh.
>
> —LUKE 6:45, EMPHASIS ADDED

The Word of God is eternal

Eternal means something everlasting; something that lasts for all time without beginning or end. Today means always current.

The Word of God is *everlasting* and will not change. *The Word of God* is current today and will always be current, tomorrow and forever and ever. *The Word of God* is dependable, it is sure and amen.

> The grass withereth, the flower fadeth: but the *word of our God* shall stand *for ever.*
>
> —ISAIAH 40:8, EMPHASIS ADDED

> Being born again...by *the word of God,* which *liveth and abideth forever.*
>
> —1 PETER 1:23, EMPHASIS ADDED

> The grass withereth, and the flower thereof falleth away: But *the word of the Lord endureth for ever.*
>
> —1 Peter 1:24–25, emphasis added

> Heaven and earth shall pass away, but *my words shall not pass away.*
>
> —Matthew 24:35, emphasis added

Jesus Tempted by Satan

We find the story of Jesus being tempted by Satan in Matthew 4:1–11 and Luke 4:1–13. What I want to bring to your attention concerning Jesus being tempted by Satan is what He used to defeat Satan. We are to follow Jesus's example, so we are to use the same method. The key words used in this passage are, "*it is written.*" I want to do an analyzation of the conversation between Satan and Jesus.

Jesus had fasted forty days and nights, and was hungry. *Satan* came to tempt Him.

> Satan said: If thou be the Son of God, command that these stones be made bread (Matt. 4:3).

> Jesus answered: *It is written*, Man shall not live by bread alone, but by every word that proceedeth out of the mouth of God (v. 4; Jesus quoted Deuteronomy 8:3).

Satan wanted *Jesus* to cast Himself down from the top of the temple.

> Satan said: If thou be the Son of God, cast thyself down: for *it is written*, He shall give his angels

> charge concerning thee: and in their hands they shall bear thee up, lest at any time thou dash thy foot against a stone (v. 6; Satan quoted Psalm 91:11–12). [Notice Satan quoted a scripture to Jesus. Satan knows the Word of God but he misuses it.]
>
> Jesus answered: *It is written* again, Thou shall not tempt the Lord thy God (v. 7; Jesus quoted Deuteronomy 6:16).

Satan took *Jesus* to a high mountain and showed Him the kingdom of the world.

> Satan said: All these things will I give thee, if thou wilt fall down and worship me (v. 9).
>
> Jesus answered: Get thee hence [*hence means get away from here*], Satan: for *it is written*, Thou shall worship the Lord thy God, and him only shalt thou serve (v. 10; Jesus quoted Deuteronomy 6:13).

Jesus quoted the Word of God; Jesus used the sword of the Spirit. Jesus defeated the tempter, Satan. We must hide the Word of God in our heart; our secret chamber, to defeat the foe. Remember this key verse: "For the *word of God* is *quick*, and *powerful*, and *sharper* than any two edged sword, *piercing* even to the dividing asunder of soul and spirit, and of the joints and marrow, and is a *discerner* of the thoughts and intents of the heart" (Heb. 4:12). We are champions; God's Word says so! We are dressed and armed for this battle.

Notice that Satan also quoted the Word of God to tempt Jesus. Satan knows the Word of God and he will misuse it to deceive or tempt us to sin. We need to know the Word and also understand it. Satan used deceit to cause Eve to sin in the Garden of Eden. Genesis 3:1–6, 13 relates the story. Let's take a look at the conversation between Eve and the serpent (the devil) and see how he deceived Eve.

> The serpent/devil said: Yea, hath God said *(did God say),* Ye shall not eat of every tree of the garden (v. 1)?
>
> The woman/Eve said: We may eat of the fruit of the trees of the garden: but of the fruit of the tree which is in the midst [means *center*] of the garden, God hath said, *Ye shall not eat of it, neither shall ye touch it, lest* [*lest* means in case: in order to prevent something happening] *ye die* (vv. 2–3).
>
> What God did say to Adam: Of every tree of the garden thou mayest freely eat: But of the *tree of the knowledge of good and evil, thou shalt not eat of it: for in the day that you eat thereof thou shalt surely die* (Gen. 2:16–17).
>
> The serpent/devil said: *Ye shall not surely die*: For God doth know that in the day ye eat thereof, then your eyes shall be opened, and ye shall be as gods, knowing good and evil (vv. 4–5).
>
> What the woman did: The woman *saw* that the tree was good for food, and that it was pleasant to the eyes, and a tree to be desired to make one wise, she *took* of the fruit thereof, and did *eat*, and

> gave also unto her husband with her; and he did eat (v. 6).
>
> What the woman said: The serpent *beguiled* me, and I did eat [*beguiled* means to mislead or deceive somebody] (v. 13).

We can, like Eve be deceived if we don't study God's Word and recognize when Satan is trying to deceive us. What the sword of the Spirit does for us is protect us from the fiery darts he throws at us. The Holy Spirit will guard us and warn us when we are in danger of falling for Satan's lies. No weapon formed against us shall prosper (Isa. 54:17). Our weapons are not carnal but mighty through God. In Revelation 19:11–16, one of the last battles fought is won using the sword of the Spirit.

> And his name is called *The Word of God*....And out of his mouth goeth a *sharp sword*, that with it he [Jesus] should smite the nations.
>
> —Revelation 19:13, 15, emphasis added

Praying

Most studies on the armor of God do not include *praying* as part of the armor. I feel it is another *powerful weapon* that God has given us. *Prayer, simply put, is talking to God.*

> *Praying always* with all *prayer* and *supplication in the Spirit*, and watching thereunto with all perseverance and supplication for all saints.
>
> —Ephesians 6:18, emphasis added

Prayer is very important, because how can you keep in touch with someone if you never talk to them? Since we are in spiritual warfare it is very important to keep in touch with our Chief Commander. In a carnal battle the soldiers cannot talk to their chief commander; communication goes through a chain of command. In this spiritual battle, we, as soldiers of the cross, have the privilege to stay in direct contact with our chief commander at all times. This verse in Ephesians says, "praying always." As Christian soldiers we are told to pray always and not give up.

In Luke 18:1, Jesus spoke, saying that men ought *always to pray* and not to faint. *Faint here means lose courage.*

> Pray without ceasing.
>
> —1 Thessalonians 5:17

> The *effectual fervent prayer* of righteous man *availeth* much [*avail* means to have an advantage or success in achieving something].
>
> —James 5:16, emphasis added

> But in every thing by *prayer and supplication* with thanksgiving let your requests be made known unto God.
>
> —Philippians 4:6, emphasis added

The next portion of Ephesians 6:18 says, "with all prayer and supplication in the Spirit." (Supplication means addressing of requests: the addressing of humble and sincere appeals to somebody with the power to grant them.) We are told to address our sincere appeals to the Chief Commander, who has the power to grant our requests. What a privilege we are given, to pray anytime to God, who is able to grant all our supplications.

Next Ephesians 6:18 says, "with all prayer and supplication *in the Spirit*."

> And I will *pray with the spirit*, and I will pray *with the understanding*.
>
> —1 CORINTHIANS 14:15, EMPHASIS ADDED

Pray, prayer, and praying is a big subject. I will not attempt to expand on the subject now, but I will say that praying the will of God is so important, and this we do when we pray in the Spirit. It is always God's will for us to be the winner in each and every battle we fight with the devil. Prayer is a powerful weapon God has given to us; use this weapon freely, it's your privilege.

In the next chapter we will look at a few of the *fiery darts* that Satan and the other members of the kingdom of darkness throw at us. Remember we are *dressed and armed* for the battle by God. *We will not be defeated*!

Chapter Five

FIERY DARTS

> Above all, taking the shield of faith wherewith ye shall be *able to quench* [extinguish fire: to put out a fire] *all the fiery darts of the wicked.*
>
> —Ephesians 6:16, emphasis added

Fire destroys everything in its path. The fiery darts of Satan are aimed to destroy us. Satan knows which of the fiery darts to use to destroy each of us, so the list to follow is not a complete list of all the fiery darts that Satan uses to cause us to lose faith and the battle. He knows which dart or darts affect each of us the most, and his purpose is to cause us to fall into temptation and sin. The *shield of faith* helps us to trust our defenders to protect us, lead us, and deliver us from all evil. Remember Satan tempts us all.

When the fiery darts come, what are we to do? Most of the fiery darts have to do with the choices we make every day. Decisions are a part of life, just because we are human. Remember we studied *the lust of the flesh, the lust of the eyes, and the pride of life*. We also looked at *the world* and all its lure to the pleasures of life. We are all tempted to sin by Satan; but *we can overcome temptations.*

The Bible gives us a lot of helpful information to be overcomers.

> Be *sober*, be *vigilant*; because *your adversary the devil*, as a roaring lion, walketh about, seeking whom he may devour: Whom *resist steadfast in faith*, knowing that the same afflictions are accomplished in your brethren that are in the world.
>
> —1 Peter 5:8–9, emphasis added

Sober: 1) serious and thoughtful, based on facts and rational thinking, 2) to become more serious or thoughtful.

Vigilant: 1) watchful and alert, 2) guard against danger, difficulties, or errors.

Resist: 1) stand firm against somebody or something, 2) refuse to give in to something, 3) to remain unaltered by the damaging effect.

Notice along with *resist*, the verse says *steadfast in the faith*. It is "Christ in me" that sustains me in the time of temptation, and keeps me from doing the things that are not pleasing to God.

> Resist the devil, and he will flee from you.
>
> —James 4:7

> But the God of all grace, who hath called us unto his eternal glory by Christ Jesus, after that ye have suffered a while, make you *perfect, stablish, strengthen, settle you*. To him be glory and dominion forever and ever. Amen. [So be it!]
>
> —1 Peter 5:10–11, emphasis added

Perfect: complete and whole.

This perfect is not as the world sees it. This perfect

is talking about Christ's continuing work in our lives, changing us to be like him (Christlike). It is a process, this daily growth until the time of the resurrection when we are changed to be like Him; the work of perfecting us will be complete.

Establish: 1) make stable; not changing, steady, firm, unmoving, 2) to start or set something up to continue or be permanent, 3) confirm.

Strengthen: to make stronger, more powerful, or increase in strength or power.

Settle: 1) to come to a decision about something, 2) unmovable. Note: *settle can also means establish.*

The scriptures given are to help *you begin* to dig deep in the Word of God. The Bible has a lot of information to help us defeat Satan and his force. This is a daily warfare, so search the scriptures daily. God will *perfect, establish, strengthen* and *settle you* as you grow in grace and knowledge.

Fiery Darts

Jealousy: 1) envious, 2) suspicious of rivals, 3) demanding exclusive loyalty or adherence

> For ye are *yet carnal*: for whereas there is among you *envying*, and *strife*, and *divisions*, are ye not carnal, and walk as men?
>
> —1 Corinthians 3:3, emphasis added

> For where *envying* and *strife* is, *there is confusion* and *every evil work*.
>
> —James 3:16, emphasis added

Let's look at the Parable of the Prodigal Son in Luke 15:11–32, particularly the older brother's reaction when the younger brother returned home after wasting his inheritance. The father threw a welcome home party for the younger son; and when the older brother returned home from the field and heard the sounds of a party, he got angry and refused to go in. When his father asked him why he refused to come in and celebrate, the older brother told his father: "I have worked hard, I have obeyed you but you never gave me a party." He was very jealous. The father told his oldest son, "You have always been with me, all I have is yours; it is necessary for us to celebrate the safe return of your brother. The older boy should have been happy for his brother's safe return; instead, he was jealous.

Pride: 1) satisfaction with self, 2) proper sense of own value

These two meanings are not bad, we should be proud of ourself when we accomplish something we set out to do; we should feel self-worth. But it is the next ones that are the troublemakers: *3) feeling of superiority: a haughty attitude when you feel you are better than someone else is, 4) conceit, 5) vanity.*

> [The Lord hates] a proud look.
>
> —Proverbs 6:16–17

> The fear of the Lord is to hate evil: *pride and arrogance.*
>
> —Proverbs 8:13, emphasis added

> *Pride* goeth before destruction, and an *haughty spirit* before a fall.
>
> —Proverbs 16:18, emphasis added

The opposite of being proud is to be humble. Jesus is the perfect example of this attitude. In Philippians 2:8–11, Paul writes about Jesus abasing and humbling Himself by coming to earth in the form of a human. But not only becoming a man but also to die on a cross. Verse 9 in the Amplified Version says, "Therefore [because He stooped so low] God has highly exalted Him and has freely bestowed on Him the name that is above every name."

> For whosoever *exalteth* himself shall be *abased*; and he that *humbleth* himself shall be *exalted*.
>
> —Luke 14:11, emphasis added

> *Humble yourselves* therefore under the mighty hand of *God*, that he may *exalt you* in due time.
>
> —1 Peter 5:6, emphasis added

> God resisteth the proud, but giveth grace unto the humble.
>
> —James 4:6

Hate: 1) intense hostility and aversion, 2) to have strong dislike or ill will for; loathe; despise, 3) detest; Hatred: 1) hate, 2) prejudiced hostility or animosity

> Thou shalt not hate thy brother in thine heart.
>
> —Leviticus 19:17

> But he that *hateth his brother is in darkness*, and walketh in darkness, and knoweth not whither he goeth, because that darkness hath blinded his eyes.
>
> —1 John 2:11, emphasis added

> Whosoever *hateth* his brother *is a murderer*: and ye know that *no murderer hath eternal life abiding in him*.
>
> —1 John 3:15, emphasis added

Lies: 1) to make an untrue statement with the intent to deceive, 2) to create a false or misleading impression (not telling the truth)

> [The Lord hates] a *lying tongue.*
>
> —Proverbs 6:17, emphasis added

> [The Lord hates] a false witness that *speaketh lies.*
>
> —Proverbs 6:19, emphasis added

> He that *speaketh lies* shall perish.
>
> —Proverbs 19:9, emphasis added

> *Lie not* to one another, seeing that ye have put off the old man [now that you are a new creature in Christ Jesus] with his deeds.
>
> —Colossians 3:9, emphasis added

> Wherefore *putting away lying, speak* every man *truth* with his neighbour.
>
> —Ephesians 4:25, emphasis added

Acts 5:1–11 tells the story of Ananias and his wife, Sapphira. They were supposed to sell some land and give the money to be distributed among those in need; but they kept back part of the price (v. 2). Verses 3 and 4: "But Peter said, Ananias, why has Satan filled thine heart to lie to the Holy Ghost, and to keep back part of the price of the land? While it remained (unsold), was it not thine own? And after it was sold, was it not in thine own power? Why hast thou conceived this thing in thine heart? Thou hast not lied unto men, but unto God" (emphasis added). Verse 5 says he fell down and died. Later his wife came in and she lied about the price they received for the land, and she died.

Sometimes people know we are lying, and sometimes they do not, but God always knows. Note: You can never tell just one lie—one lie leads to another.

Stealing: 1) to take secretly or without permission, 2) to seize, gain, or win by trickery—stealing is the act of one who steals

Stealing should make a person feel guilty.

> *Let him that stole steal no more*: but rather let him labor, working with his hands the thing which is good, that he may have to give to him that needeth.
> —Ephesians 4:28, emphasis added

> Thou shall not steal.
> —Exodus 20:15

This is one of the Ten Commandments. The Ten Commandments were given to Moses before Christ became our Savior. When Jesus was on earth, He quoted and emphasized some of them. (See Matthew 19:18–19.) There are even laws in our land that punish people who steal.

We all know the story of Zacchaeus, who climbed a sycamore tree in order to see Jesus as He was walking by. Jesus went to his house as a guest, but the people who heard Jesus invite himself murmured that Jesus was going as a guest to a sinner's house. This has a good ending because in Luke 19:8 we find what Zacchaeus said: "And Zacchaeus stood, and said unto the Lord: Behold, Lord, the half of my goods I give to the poor; *and if I have taken any thing from any man by false accusation, I restore him fourfold*" (emphasis added). Zacchaeus made restitution and Jesus told him *that salvation had come to his house today.* He chose to do as Ephesians 4:28 said to do: "Let him that stole steal no more."

Disobedience: 1) refusal or neglect to obey, 2) fail to obey—to be disobedient, especially if habitually

> For as by *one man's disobedience many were made sinners*, so by the *obedience of one shall many be made righteous.*
>
> —Romans 5:19, emphasis added

This scripture is talking about the disobedience of Adam in the garden. It brought sin into the lives of mankind. Adam is not the only person whose disobedience has affected the lives of mankind; we all affect each other's lives. Not in the great way Adam's disobedience did, but we still affect each other when we are disobedient to God's Word. The second part of this scripture says: "by the obedience of one (Jesus) shall many be made righteous." Read John 17:4–11: Jesus gave His life that all of mankind could be reconciled to God the Father. What is wonderful, Jesus is still redeeming mankind and will be until He comes again.

Moses was not allowed to enter the Promised Land because of *disobedience*; he hit the rock instead of speaking to it. (Read Numbers 20:7–12.) This rock in the Old Testament represents Jesus as our coming Savior. (Read 1 Corinthians 10:4.) Jesus was going to be crucified once and for all; for all people; but when Moses, angry at the people, hit the rock, he disobeyed God's command to speak to it. In 1 Corinthians 10:1–6, God told him because of his *disobedience* he could not enter the Promised Land. Before Moses died, God did show him the Promised Land: "And the Lord said unto him, This is the land which I sware unto Abraham, unto Isaac, and unto Jacob, saying, I will give it unto thy seed: I have caused thee to see it with thine eyes, but thou shalt not go over thither [*in the direction of that place*]" (Deut. 34:4). *Disobedience* always has a consequence.

Covet: 1) to wish for enviously, 2) to desire another's possessions; long for with envy, 3) have a craving for possessions, 4) greedy

> *Thou shall not covet*...any thing that is thy neighbor's.
>
> —Exodus 20:17, emphasis added

This is another one of the Ten Commandments. In order for us not be covetous we have to get our priorities straight.

> For we brought nothing into this world, and it is certain we can carry nothing out.
>
> —1 Timothy 6:7

> Let your conversation *be without covetousness; and be content with such things as ye have.*
>
> —Hebrews 13:5, emphasis added

> [Jesus] said unto them, Take heed, and *beware of covetousness*: for a man's life consisteth not in the abundance of the things which he possesseth.
>
> —Luke 12:15, emphasis added

After Jesus made the statement about covetousness, He told a parable about a rich man whose land yielded more than he had room for; he pulled down his barns and built larger ones to hold all his produce.

Then he said, "I have enough goods to last many years, now I can rest, eat, drink, and be merry." But God said, "Tonight your soul shall be required of you and then who shall those things belong to?" We as Christians must put God first and then all the things we need He will provide. The big problem with this man: he was *greedy*. This parable is found in Luke 12:15–21.

Cursing: 1) to use profane language, 2) a swearword, obscenity, or blasphemous oath

> But now I write to you *not to associate with anyone who bears the name of* [*Christian*] *brother* if he is known to be guilty of immorality or greed, or is an idolater [whose soul is devoted to any object that usurps the place of God] or is a person with a *foul tongue* [*railing, abusing, reveling, slandering*], or is a drunkard or a swindler or a robber. [No] *you must not so much as eat with such a person.*
>
> —1 Corinthians 5:11, amp, emphasis added

> Out of the *same mouth proceedeth blessings and cursing*. My brethren, these things *ought not so to be*.
>
> —James 3:10, emphasis added

> But now ye also *put off all these*; anger, wrath, malice, blasphemy, *filthy communication out of your mouth*.
>
> —Colossians 3:8, emphasis added

> If any man among you seem to be religious, and *bridleth not his tongue, but deceiveth his own heart, this man's religion is vain.*
>
> —James 1:26, emphasis added

Blasphemy: 1) disrespect for God or sacred things, 2) showing disrespect for God or sacred things

> But now ye also put off all these; anger, wrath, malice, *blasphemy, filthy communication out of your mouth.*
>
> —COLOSSIANS 3:8, EMPHASIS ADDED

> Let no corrupt communication proceed out of your mouth: but that which is good to the use of edifying that it may minister grace unto the hearers [edify means: to instruct or improve morally or spiritually].
>
> —EPHESIANS 4:29

Exodus 20:7 says, "Thou shall not take the name of the Lord thy God in vain" (vain = that is, lightly or frivolously, in false affirmation or profanely) (emphasis added). This is the third commandment.

Worldly Things: 1) experienced in and knowledgeable about human society and its ways, 2) relating to everyday material existence, 3) materialistic: much more interested in everyday materialistic concerns than in the spiritual side of life

> Love not the world, neither the things that are in the world. If any man love the world, the love of the Father is not in him.
>
> —1 JOHN 2:15

> And *be not conformed to this world*: but be ye transformed by the *renewing of your mind*, that ye may prove what is that *good*, and *acceptable*, and *perfect, will of God.*
>
> —ROMANS 12:2, EMPHASIS ADDED

The word conformed in this verse means: 1) don't follow the world's standard, 2) don't be similar; which is not to shape or pattern your life after the world.

Cheating: 1) deception—to be deceiving, 2) break rules to gain an unfair advantage, 3) dishonest or unfair trick

Dishonest: not honest or truthful; meaning to deceive, trick, or defraud people

> Keep thy tongue from evil, and thy lips from speaking guile [*guile means; deceitful or tricky*].
>
> —Psalm 34:13

> Wherefore laying aside all malice, and all *guile*, and hypocrisies, and envies, and all evil speakings.
>
> —1 Peter 2:1, emphasis added

First Corinthians 6:1–8 (amp) goes so far as to say even if one of your fellow Christians was to defraud (defraud means cheat somebody) you, don't take them to a court of law. It is better for you to take a loss. That's pretty strong. Verse 10 says cheaters (swindlers and thieves)...shall not inherit the kingdom of God. The opposite of dishonest is truthful. Jesus is the way, the truth and the life. We know that Jesus would never cheat or be dishonest, so we cannot allow Satan to deceive us into cheating in any form or to be dishonest.

Bad entertainment is anything that is against the principles of God; that which promotes bad behavior and lustful desires

> Forasmuch then as Christ hath suffered for us in the flesh, arm yourselves likewise with the same

> mind: for he that hath suffered in the flesh hath ceased from sin; *That he no longer should live the rest of his time in the flesh to the lusts of men,* but to the will of God. For the time past of our life may suffice us to have wrought the will of the Gentiles, when we *walked in lasciviousness, lusts, excess of wine, revellings, banquetings, and abominable idolatries.*
>
> —1 PETER 4:1–3, EMPHASIS ADDED

- *Lasciviousness* means indecent, provoking lust.
- *Revellings* are noisy celebrations usually involving, eating, drinking, dancing, and noise.
- *Idolatries* means extreme admiration for someone or something.

This scripture gives a list of the types of entertainment and actions that Christians cannot participate in. If it promotes lust, drinking, indecency, and idolatries, we are to avoid such places and people who promote these actions. First Peter 4:4 reads, "Wherein they [friends] think it strange that ye run not with them [friends] to the same excess of riot, speaking evil of you" (emphasis added). The Amplified Version of this verse reads: "They are astonished and think it very queer that you do not now run hand in hand with them in the same excesses of dissipation [overindulgence in the pursuit of physical pleasures], and they abuse [you]" (emphasis added).

Drinking: excessive consumption of alcohol; drunkard

Drugs: illegal substance: an often illegal and sometimes addictive substance that causes changes in behavior and perception and is taken for the effects

> But now I write to you *not to associate with anyone who bears the name of* [*Christian*] *brother,* if he is known to be guilty of immorality or greed, or is an idolater [whose soul is devoted to any object that usurps the place of God] or is a person with a *foul tongue* [*railing, abusing, reviling, slandering*], or is *a drunkard* or a *swindler or a robber.* [No] *you must not so much as eat with such a person.*
>
> —1 CORINTHIANS 5:11, AMP, EMPHASIS ADDED

> Let us walk honestly, as in the day; not in *rioting* [*The Amplified Version uses carousing which means to drink and become noisy: especially in a group*] and *drunkenness,* not in chambering and wantonness, not in strife and envying. But put ye on the Lord Jesus Christ, and make not provision for the flesh, to fulfill the lusts thereof.
>
> —ROMANS 13:13–14, EMPHASIS ADDED

I have given definitions, scriptures, and a few comments. May I suggest you look closely at the meanings, as the meanings in themselves explain why they are not pleasing traits or habits for us to have. I am including this chapter in the hope that it will help you understand how Satan can use these actions to trip us up and bring sin into our hearts. This is not a conclusive list, but these are the ones that we as humans have trouble with the most. I also realize that all these words are not written in the Bible exactly like I have presented them, but the Scriptures are clear about what is pleasing to God and what is not. My personal opinion on this subject is this: If you have to argue your point, what is the point? In our hearts, we know right from wrong. Follow after God—that means chase after Him—and you will not have time to question what you can and cannot do. Remember we can also obtain a seared conscience, so pray and keep praying. God will see you through this spiritual battle to victory!

Overcomers Are Winners

There is one more word that I want us to look at closer, and that is *overcome*. I said at the beginning of this chapter *we can overcome temptations*. What does it mean to *overcome*? *Overcome means 1) one that defeats somebody, especially in conflict. 2) to win despite obstacles, 3) conquer. Synonym: defeat: 1) beat enemy: to win a victory over enemy forces in a battle or war.*

How do we *overcome* the enemy? Put on the whole armor of God and stand firm in His Word. Another way to overcome is found in Romans 12:21: "Be not overcome of evil, but overcome evil with good." In Revelation chapters 2 and 3 are messages to seven churches. After the Holy Spirit tells each church what they are doing right and what they are doing wrong, there is a promise given to them. These promises are to every believer.

The Seven Promises to Him That Overcomes

1. "To him that *overcometh* will I give to *eat of the tree of life*, which is in the midst of the paradise of God" (Rev. 2:7).

2. "He that overcometh shall not be hurt of the second death" (2:11).
3. "To him that overcometh will I give to eat of the hidden manna, and will give him a white stone, and in the stone a new name written, which no man knoweth saving he that receiveth it" (2:17).
4. "And he that overcometh, and keepeth my works unto the end, to him will I give power over the nations…and I will give him the morning star" (2:26, 28).
5. "He that overcometh, the same shall be clothed in white raiment (*dress same as clothing*); and I will not blot out his name out of the book of life, but I will confess his name before my Father, and before his angels" (3:5).
6. "Him that overcometh will I make a pillar in the temple of my God, and he shall go no more out: and I will write upon him the name of my God, and the name of the city of my God, which is new Jerusalem, which cometh down out of heaven from my God: and I will write upon him my new name" (3:12).
7. "To him that overcometh will I grant to sit with me in my throne, even as I also overcome, and am set down with my Father in his throne" (3:21).

What wonderful promises given to us who overcome the onslaught (overwhelming assault or force: a powerful attack or force that overwhelms somebody or a very large amount of things that are hard to deal with) of the enemy. We can trust God to help us to overcome for two reasons: 1) God would never make promises to us if it wasn't possible for us to overcome the enemy, and win this battle. 2) God gave us a perfect example by sending His Son to earth.

> For even to this were you called [it is inseparable from your vocation]. *For Christ also suffered for you, leaving you [His personal] example, so that you should follow on in His footsteps.* He was guilty of no sin, neither was deceit (guile) ever found on His lips. When He was reviled and insulted, He did not revile or offer insult in return; [when] He was abused and suffered, He made no threats [of vengeance]; but He trusted [Himself and everything] to Him Who judges fairly. He personally bore our sins in His [own] body to the tree [as on an altar and offered Himself on it], that we might die (cease to exist) to sin and live to righteousness.
>
> —1 Peter 2:21–24, AMP, EMPHASIS ADDED

> Whoever says he abides in Him ought [as a personal debt] to walk and conduct himself in the same way in which He walked and conducted Himself.
>
> —1 John 2:6, AMP

> Let no man despise thy youth; but be thou an example of the believers, in word [speech], in conversation [conduct], in charity [love], in spirit, in faith, in purity.
>
> —1 Timothy 4:12

Note: The words in brackets are from the Amplified Version of the Bible.

Then we can say, like Paul, "I have fought a good fight, I have finished my course, I have kept the faith: Henceforth there is laid up for me a crown of righteousness, which the Lord, the righteous judge, shall give me at that day: and not to me only, but unto all them also that love his appearing" (2 Tim. 4:7–8).

This battle is not easy to fight, but remember: *If God be for us, who can be against us? And "Greater is He that is within me than he that is in the world." We are winners*!

Chapter Six

A WARRIOR'S PRAYER

Author Unknown

(For a more in depth prayer, go to http://crupress.campuscrusadeforchrist.com/green/_assets/crucomm/bubecktoolsforwarfare.pdf)

I am grateful, heavenly Father, that the Lord Jesus Christ triumphed over all principalities and dark powers. I claim that victory for my life today. I reject all the accusations and temptations of Satan. I affirm that the Word of God is true and I choose to live today in the light of His Word. Open my eyes and show me the areas of my life that do not please You. Work in me to cleanse me from all ground that would give Satan a foothold against me.

I am thankful that You have made a provision so that today I can live filled with the Spirit of God, with love and joy and peace, with long-suffering, gentleness and goodness, with meekness, faithfulness and self-control in my life. I recognize that this is your will for me and so I reject and resist all the endeavors of Satan and his wicked spirits to rob me of the will of God.

In my own life today I tear down the strongholds of Satan and smash the plans of Satan that have been formed against me. I tear down the strongholds of Satan against my mind, and I surrender my mind to You, blessed Holy Spirit. I affirm, heavenly Father, that you have not given me the spirit of fear, but of power and of love and of a sound mind. I break and smash the strongholds of Satan formed against my emotions today and I give my emotions to You. I smash the strongholds of Satan formed against my will today; I give my will to You and choose to make the right decisions of faith. I smash the strongholds of Satan formed against my body today. I give my body to You recognizing that I am Your temple. I rejoice in Your mercy and goodness.

Heavenly Father, I pray that now and through this day You would strengthen and enlighten me, show me the way Satan is hindering and tempting and lying and distorting the truth in my life.

I cover myself with the blood of the Lord Jesus Christ and pray that You, blessed Holy Spirit, would bring all the work of the crucifixion, all the work of the resurrection, all the work of the glorification and the work of Pentecost into my life today.

In Jesus's name, amen.

ABOUT THE AUTHOR

KATHLEEN NELSON WAS BORN IN Jennings, Louisiana, and moved to Dallas, Texas, as a young bride, where she has resided ever since. Because of her love of God's Word, she began teaching a Sunday school class when she was fifteen years old and has continued to teach the Bible every chance she gets. The Bible is the most interesting book and she never gets tired of searching for the "gold nuggets" it contains. For Kathleen, the opportunity to write studies about this wonderful book is a dream come true. Her prayer is that everyone who reads *Spiritual Warfare* will grow to love the Bible as she does.

CONTACT THE AUTHOR

WWW.KATHLEEN-NELSON.COM